DEWEY AND
BEHAVIORISTIC
CONTEXT
OF ETHICS

DONALD MORRIS

DEWEY AND BEHAVIORISTIC CONTEXT OF ETHICS

DONALD MORRIS

International Scholars Publications
San Francisco - London - Bethesda
1996

Library of Congress Cataloging-in-Publication Data

Morris, Donald, 1945-
    Dewey and the behavioristic context of ethics / Donald Morris.
      p. cm.
    Includes bibliographical references and index.
    ISBN 1-57309-041-7 (cloth : alk. paper). -- ISBN 1-57309-040-9
    (pbk. : alk. paper)
    1. Dewey, John, 1859-1952--Ethics. I. Title.
    B945.D4M67   1996
    171'.2--dc20   96-26388
                                                  CIP

Editorial Inquiries:
International Scholars Publications
7831 Woodmont Avenue, #345
Bethesda, MD 20814

To order: (800) 55-PUBLISH

Among those in the vortex of continua which produced this treatise I would like to acknowledge Professor S. Morris Eames of Southern Illinois University, Carbondale and my children Keith and Sarah. They have greatly extended the meaning of this project.

ꙮ

TABLE OF CONTENTS

❧

DEWEY AND THE PROBLEM OF ETHICS AND PSYCHOLOGY

1. Statement of Problem and Purpose of the Study

This study is an examination of the problem of the relation of ethics to psychology in John Dewey's philosophy. Dewey contends that before one can accurately define the scope and purpose of ethics or moral theory and before one can evaluate moral problems, all relevant suppositions concerning human nature must be made explicit and brought into agreement with the best available conclusions of psychology. The way this contention of Dewey's is worked out in his psychology and ethics forms the theme of this study.

Dewey's views on the nature of scientific explanation and its relations to ethics will be examined. Given Dewey's position concerning the philosophy of science, it will be shown that a behavioristic philosophy of psychology represents a natural development of his thought. The concept of behaviorism will be explored briefly in its early version as set forth by John B. Watson, and more fully in its later form as expressed in the radical behaviorism of B. F. Skinner. Dewey's criticisms of Watsonian behaviorism are similar to those of Skinner, and it will be seen that a number of similarities exist between Dewey and Skinner with respect to psychological theory, to the need for a psychological grounding of ethical theory, and to the psychological and ethical basis of social reform.

At the core of Dewey's philosophical thinking is the conviction that inquiry into a subject is evoked by an indeterminate situation. Such a situation is characterized by ambiguity, confusion, obscurity, and conflicting tendencies.[1] When a situation marked by these features is seen to require inquiry and resolution, it is labeled a "problematic situation" by

Dewey.[2] In his writings, Dewey expresses the belief that the artificial separation which exists between individually experienced moral problems, on the one hand, and moral or ethical theory in its philosophical, religious, and common sense manifestations, on the other hand, constitutes just such a subject of needed inquiry and resolution.

In sorting out the elements which give rise to this difficulty or problematic situation, Dewey argues that the existence of moral theory itself can be traced to an earlier source of confusion and obscurity: the attempt by the ancient Greeks "to find a regulation for the conduct of life which should have a rational basis and purpose instead of being derived from customs."[3] According to Dewey, the attempt of the Greeks to discover a rational basis for moral action led to the founding of several conceptual dichotomies, which were instrumental in producing the aforementioned split between moral theory and practice. One dichotomy was the general distinction between knowledge and action, which had its basis in Greek social and cultural conditions.[4] For the Greek philosophers, "practical activity is dismissed to a world of low grade reality," according to Dewey, and thus "one must go to passionless reason to find perfect reality and complete certitude."[5] The problem which this position poses for Dewey is that "theory separated from concrete doing and making is empty and futile; practice then becomes an immediate seizure of opportunities and enjoyments which conditions afford without the direction which theory—knowledge and ideas—has power to supply."[6]

In addition to the distinction between theory and practice, Dewey notes other dichotomies pioneered by the Greeks which have had a bearing on the development of moral thought: the Good (or goodness) divided into instrumental (means) and intrinsic (fixed ends),[7] conduct divided into actions with moral import and those without,[8] and the actual in opposition to the ideal.[9] These dichotomies, along with others of more general scope (including rational-empirical, subjective-objective, being-becoming, change-permanence, and mind-nature), fused together to form the conceptual framework by means of which much of the Western philosophical tradition has developed.[10] Within the framework of these conceptions, philosophers historically have waged battles with one another over the correct view of the moral life.

For Dewey, finding the correct view, however, must begin with a loosening of the rigidity with which these dichotomies are held, and this begins with the distinction between theory and practice. Without a rethinking of the basis of moral theory, the lack of authentic progress in this area (which has led some philosophers in the twentieth century to declare ethics bankrupt and moral statements meaningless) will become more dramatic, particularly when seen against the background of the developments in the natural and social sciences. To overcome the apparent lack of progress in ethical theory, Dewey suggests that the effective logical methods which have allowed science to progress to its present state must be integrated into ethical theory. Dewey took it upon himself to pursue this task. Hence, as a recurrent theme in his writings, he regularly attacks the dichotomies mentioned above. He traces them to their intellectual sources and shows how, even after the social and scientific conditions which had given rise to them had vanished, philosophers had held fast to the conceptions involved and often had imputed them to the nature of the world itself. These dichotomies are often seen as rigid categories to be worked within, rather than recognized as once useful instruments whose utility had faded with the growth and development of science and the evolution of new social institutions.

In the place of these anachronistic conceptions, Dewey attempts to reconstruct moral theory in line with principles of sound scientific method. He begins, for example, by going back to the original data of moral theory, namely, individual moral problems. Rather than determining general moral standards and then attempting to make them apply to individual situations, Dewey believes one must begin with the individual situations themselves. Thus Dewey says:

> The transfer of the burden of the moral life from following rules or pursuing fixed ends over to the detection of the ills that need remedy in a special case and the formation of plans and methods for dealing with them, eliminates the causes which have kept moral theory controversial, and which have also kept it remote from helpful contact with the exigencies of practice.[11]

In addition to the rejection of rigid moral rules and fixed ends or goods, Dewey stresses that, as in scientific inquiry generally, ethical theory and practice must be seen as mutually supportive. Dewey also broadens the traditional realm of morally significant action. He argues that potentially any action can have moral significance when considered in relation to its consequences. Finally, moral judgments, for Dewey, are to be treated as hypotheses to be tested in practice, and moral theory generally is to be brought into line with current developments in the sciences. For example, rather than allowing moral decisions to be made in the context of pre-scientific and common sense conceptions of human nature, Dewey recognizes that ethics must operate in the context of the best available scientific knowledge. This is seen as especially true in the case of the social sciences, and among them psychology in particular, since, in dealing with the prescriptive limitations of conduct, one must work within the descriptive limitations of behavior. On this point Dewey says:

> Evaluative judgments cannot be arrived at so as to be warranted without going outside the "value field" into matters physical, physiological, anthropological, historical, socio-psychological, and so on. Only by taking facts ascertained in these subjects into account can we determine the conditions and consequences of given valuings, and without such determination "judgment" occurs only as pure myth.[12]

In the 1932 *Ethics,* Dewey further indicates the need for basing ethics on scientific knowledge. There he says:

> To give a scientific account of judgments about conduct, means to find the principles which are the basis of these judgments. Conduct or the moral life has two obvious aspects. On the one hand it is a life of purpose. It implies thought and feeling, ideals and motives, valuation and choice. These are processes to be studied by psychological methods. On the other hand, conduct has its outward side. It has relations to nature, and especially to human society. Moral life is called out or stimulated by certain necessities of individual and social existence.... These relations to nature and society are studied by the biological and social sciences. Sociology, economics, politics, law, and jurisprudence deal particularly with this aspect of conduct. Ethics must employ their methods and results for this aspect of its problem, as it employs psychology for the examination of conduct on its inner side.[13]

Historically, there has been a connection between various philosophers' conceptions of human nature or psychology and their ethical theories. Plato stresses the importance of directing the conduct of our lives toward a goal of psychological integration and harmony among the distinguishable factors of our mental constitution. Aristotle holds that the excellence of our moral lives can be measured against the extent to which we act in our specifically human capacity, that is, as rational beings. Through an examination of our natural tendencies, St. Thomas Aquinas teaches that we can discover the principles of conduct by which God intended us to reach our highest mode of existence. For Kant, it is our nature as rational beings which dictates the principle against which we are bound to gauge the moral significance of our actions. Bentham bases his moral prescriptions on what he takes to be the universal desire within human nature for pleasure. These examples can be expanded, but their point already should be clear. What philosophers have taken human nature to be has influenced the content of their moral theories.

Since Wilhelm Wundt's experimental school and the emergence of psychology as an experimental science, however, the necessity for moral philosophers to correct their psychological presuppositions and to align them with current developments in psychological theory has become crucial. Many contemporary ethical theorists have been slow to recognize that the effectiveness of ethical thought is, at least to some extent, at the mercy of the accuracy of what are taken to be the facts of human psychological life.[14]

Dewey adheres to the idea that ethics can be effective only when it takes the psychological conditions of human nature seriously and builds upon them as a base. For Dewey, conduct which is moral and conduct which is guided by intelligence are merely two appellations for the same phenomenon—viewed from alternate perspectives.[15] Intelligent direction of our conduct implies a knowledge of the conditions and consequences of our thoughts and actions, including their psychological aspects. Thus, in *Human Nature and Conduct*, Dewey says that "the problem of the place of knowledge and judgment in conduct depends upon getting the fundamental psychology of thought straightened out."[16]

When the relation between ethics and psychology is seen in the context of the growth and development of each, it becomes apparent that, as psychology develops, moral theory must be developed also. One of the most dramatic developments in psychological theory has been the transition from a generally introspective focus and method (psychology as a study of mind or consciousness) to methods and perspectives emphasizing behavior. Behavior is seen not as an interaction of inner and outer selves, but as a unified totality. The latter view of behavior as the topic of psychological investigation makes data available for study which were not thought directly relevant to our understanding of human nature by the former introspective view. These data include outward, observable manifestations of behavior, its biological and physiological determinants, as well as its potentialities and limitations as traced from the evolutionary development of the species in question. Central to this transition has been the rejection by some psychologists, for example, B. F. Skinner, of explanations of behavior relying on purely mentalistic terms. Skinner rejects the prospect of explaining human behavior in terms of the "free" choices of an autonomous inner "mind" or "mental agent." His reason for so doing is not primarily metaphysical or epistemological; rather, it is pragmatic. According to Skinner:

> Mentalistic explanations allay curiosity and bring inquiry to a stop. It is so easy to observe feelings and states of mind at a time and in a place which make them seem like causes that we are not inclined to inquire further.[17]

Skinner's position on this matter is similar to that of Dewey. In an article entitled "How is Mind to be Known?" Dewey criticizes attempts to understand mental life through introspection and "indubitable immediate knowledge" on the grounds that this method "eliminates, once and for all, the need for reflection and inquiry."[18] For Skinner, as well as for Dewey, then, the psychological viewpoint which will ultimately prove most useful in understanding problems of the control and prediction of human behavior will be one which bypasses explanations which rest in "the purely mental." Instead, for both men, explanations of behavior must be given in terms which give rise to observable data, experimentation, and inquiry. Although this shift in method from a mentalistic and introspective basis of explanation to a behavioristic one is commonplace in psychology, it has been slow to take effect in much of philosophical and common sense thought. The concept of an autonomous inner self or mind-as-agent represents a long standing tradition in Western philosophical thought; look only to the metaphysical concept of the dualistic person having a mind and a body. Dewey points out: "We are only just now commencing to appreciate how completely exploded is the psychology that dominated philosophy throughout the eighteenth and nineteenth centuries."[19]

2. Behaviorism

In general, behaviorism, as the term will be used in the present work, refers not to a body of conclusions or doctrines, but to an attitude toward or perspective upon the study of human behavior. George Herbert Mead, who called himself a "social behaviorist," says that "behaviorism... is simply an approach to the study of experience of the individual from the point of view of his conduct, particularly, but not exclusively, the conduct as it is observed by others."[20] B. F. Skinner said of behaviorism that:

> It does not deny the possibility of self-observation or self-knowledge or its possible usefulness, but it questions the nature of what is felt or observed and hence known. It restores introspection [in opposition to Watson's behaviorism] but not what philosophers and introspective psychologists had believed they were "specting," and it raises questions of how much of one's own body one can actually observe.[21]

Behaviorism, then, in the general sense which covers both Skinner and Dewey, is a philosophy of psychology, not a psychological doctrine. As Skinner points out, "behaviorism is not the science of human behavior; it is the philosophy of that science."[22] It is characterized by (1) an emphasis on correlations of behavior forms or patterns with environmental conditions, and (2) an interest in determining the meaning of behavior by reference to the history of the interactions of the organism with its environment. In examining this history of interactions, the focus of attention is placed upon the consequences of past behavior as determinants of future behavior. That is, for both Dewey and Skinner, the meaning of an act is equivalent to its connections with other acts, both past and future, and the consequences of these acts, both actual and probable. The antimentalistic posture of behaviorism is to be understood in the context of the history of the unspectacular attempts by psychologists and philosophers to account for behavior on purely mental principles. The hope is that by getting beyond immediate feelings and seeking correlations of observable events, not only explanation, but prediction and control of behavior will become possible.

Finally, in addition to what has been said already about behaviorism, it should be noted that behaviorism uses the biological evolution of organisms as a relevant consideration in accounting for certain aspects of behavior, especially those concerned with abilities and predilections toward being affected by certain aspects of the environment in specific ways. This accounts for the use in much of behavioristic psychology of animal experimentation. The underlying supposition is that differences between species, for some purposes, may be less important than similarities when the evolutionary histories of the species can be traced to common ancestry.

With the growing influence and importance of the general behavioristic point of view in current psychological theory and the subsequent need to make correlative adjustments in ethical theory, Dewey's related work takes on increasing importance for the field of ethics. As will be shown in Chapter Five of this study, new light may be thrown on many current ethical problems by relating the ethical concepts in question to relevant psychological conditions involved in the production of the problems. This will be true in the case of both normative questions and so-called recta-ethical problems, for instance, the "is-ought" controversy.

In the Chapters which follow, Dewey's views on psychology and ethics and their interrelations will be set forth. Particular emphasis will be placed on the behavioristic aspects of Dewey's mature ethical and psychological writings. The fourth chapter will present the ethical views of B.F. Skinner in the context of his behavioristic psychology. Skinner's views will then be compared with those of Dewey. In the latter discussion it will be argued that Dewey correctly emphasizes the need for reconstruction in ethical theory and, also sees that this construction must begin by taking stock of the best available evidence concerning human behavior.

3. Ethics and Science

Before turning to these considerations, however, it is important to understand the more general context of Dewey's position on the relation of ethics to psychology. This context is Dewey's view of the relation between ethics and science. An outline of this more generic correspondence will afford a basis by which the more particular problem of the relationship between ethics and the science of human behavior can be brought into clearer perspective.

More than once in his writings, Dewey stated that it is in the attempt to relate the things we value to the results of scientific inquiry that philosophy is to find its most important task.[23] For example, in the *Quest for Certainty* he says:

> Man has beliefs which scientific inquiry vouchsafes, beliefs about the actual structure and processes of things; and he also has beliefs about the values which should regulate his conduct. The question of how these two ways of believing may most effectively and fruitfully interact with one another is the most general and significant of all the problems which life presents to us. Some reasoned discipline, one obviously other than any science, should deal with this issue. Thus there is supplied one way of conceiving the function of philosophy.[24]

Although always aware that this relationship is one of the central problems with which philosophy is faced, Dewey did not always take the same stand towards its resolution. In an 1887 article entitled "Ethics and Physical Science," Dewey sets forth two opposing views concerning the proper basis of ethics. His own choice saw the correct foundation for ethics to be theological, rather than scientific. The other view presented was criticized by Dewey because it based ethics on a "physical interpretation of the universe ... which necessarily shuts out those ideas and principles which are fundamental to ethics."[25] The latter point of view, which has a strong Spencerian cast to it: (see page 10) claims that "science has discovered the law of evolution; this law shows the universe making towards a certain end," and asks: "What higher object, indeed, what other object of human action can be conceived than conformity with the law of all existence?"[26] This point of view, according to Dewey, is "the especial contention of men of science who have turned their thoughts to the sphere of moral action." It is the contention of these scientists that "they are putting ethics, for the first time, on a scientific basis, and giving to it a positive sanction and a positive end."[27]

In contrast to this view, Dewey describes his own position. For example, in reference to his own belief that science considered as a purely physical description of the universe is not capable of grounding ethics, Dewey states: "We believe that the cause of theology and morals is one, and that whatever banishes God from the heart of things, with the same edict excludes the ideal, the ethical, from the life of man."[28] In support of his point of view, Dewey describes three basic arguments against using physical science as a basis for grounding ethics.

The first argument has to do with three traits he considers necessary conditions of moral reasoning, but which are incompatible with a scientific view of ethics. These three traits are part of an analysis of human choice and include: (1) activity for a purpose or end, (2) activity from personal choice, and (3) activity directed toward an ideal.[29] Dewey's reason for holding that a scientifically based moral theory is incapable of dealing with these concepts is his assumption that principles of science are fundamentally mechanical. That is, the universe described from a scientific point of view leaves no room for purpose, choice, or ideals because its mechanical laws attempt to account for all phenomena on the basis of prior physical conditions and uniformities. As will become apparent in the discussion below, Dewey was later able to change his position regarding the relation of science and ethics by altering his conception of the ways in which science explains or describes the physical universe.

The second of Dewey's arguments against basing ethics on a foundation of science seems to be directed against Herbert Spencer, or at least against the general Spencerian point of view. It is part of Spencer's contention that the evolutionary process is leading eventually to a harmony or unity of purpose. This harmony must grow out of a disharmony or struggle leading to the "survival of the fittest." For Dewey this is more than "merely a logical or dialectical difficulty in the theory, which may be got over by a readjustment of statement. On the contrary," he says, "it appears...to touch the fundamental fallacy of physical ethics."[30] The problem, according to Dewey, is that Spencer, or a propounder of that form of ethical theory, has got the situation backwards. For Dewey, whereas "it *is* necessary for the physical moralist to show that the natural process can produce a community of interest, a good which does not admit of competition, one which belongs with equal right to all,"[31] in actuality "he begins by assuming that moral order which he professes to explain."[32]

The cause of this apparent attempt by Spencer to begin by assuming what he intended to demonstrate, can be traced to an ambiguity to which Dewey continued to draw attention throughout his later writings. This ambiguity concerns the term 'end,' which may mean 'end-in-view' or 'final close.' In his 1938 *Logic: The Theory of Inquiry,* for example, Dewey says: "The end-in-view of the man who sees an automobile approaching him is *getting to* a place of safety, not safety itself. The latter (or its opposite) is the *end* in the sense of close."[33] Although Dewey had not adopted the term 'end-in-view' in "Ethics and Physical Science," he makes the point against Spencer quite clearly when he says:

> The term "end" when we speak of the universe means its last term, the direction towards which it is actually tending; the term "end" when we speak of the ethical end of man means the goal to which he is to direct his attention, that to which he is, so far as in him lies, to give reality.[34]

Thus the difficulty with the physical moralists is that, although they deny purposiveness *as such* in nature, they introduce the ethical idea of purpose into their system through the ambiguity of the term 'end'.[35]

Dewey's third argument against the physical moralist's reasoning deals with the topic of logically deriving what ought to be from what is. Here Dewey's point is that, even were he to concede that the pattern of evolution could be discerned and that it could be predicted with accuracy in what direction mankind's evolution will continue, this information would still remain on the level of fact and give us no direct obligation. The *ought* in the situation has to be introduced by human choice and cannot be discovered in the situation. Thus Dewey states that since

> an end which is *man's* end, whether ethical or not, must
> be one which he has himself the power of realizing;....
> It is not enough that there be an end which is worked out
> through man as an instrument; man must himself work
> out this end.[36]

This latter point may be analyzed into two important considerations, both of which recur in Dewey's later writings.

The first is that, while facts are necessary in order to make effective decision, the facts never interpret themselves. A human agent must always "do something" with the facts. In 1929, for example, in *The Quest for Certainty,* Dewey says:

> To say that something is enjoyed is to make a statement
> about a fact, something already in existence; it is not to
> judge the value of that fact .... To call an object a value
> is to assert that it satisfies or fulfills certain conditions.
> Function and status in meeting conditions is a different
> matter from bare existence. The fact that something is
> desired only raises the *question* of its desirability; it
> does not settle it.[37]

The second point is one which is of ultimate importance in Dewey's later arguments that ethics must be grounded in psychology. It can be stated in its simplest form in the dictum "ought implies can"; or, in interrogative form, as when Dewey asks: "Can it be laid down as the ultimate law of human conduct: Thou shalt make thyself a means towards an end in which thou has neither part nor lot?"[38] As will be discussed below, it became of great importance to Dewey that we know the specific limitations within which ethical considerations are to be formulated. For Dewey, the questions of morals must undergo constant reevaluation in the light of ever growing scientific knowledge; that is, what constitutes the "ought" is subject to change as we continue to discover more and more about the "is" of human nature. Dewey amplifies this point in his 1932 *Ethics,* where he says:

> At present biologists, psychologists, and sociologists
> are far from agreement as to the relative part played in

the individual's makeup and character by heredity, environment, and the individual's own choices and habits. Similarly in the history of races and cultures, the importance of race, of economic and other social forces, and of great men, is variously estimated by anthropologists, historians, and other students of this complex problem. For our purpose we shall assume that all these factors enter into moral growth, although it may some times be convenient to distinguish what nature does, what society does, and what the individual does for himself, as he chooses, thinks, selects, and forms habits and character.[39]

In statement, if not intent, Dewey's later views concerning science's relationship to ethics show a marked contrast to his earlier position as just outlined. This relationship is by no means simple. Dewey discusses at least four ways in which the two areas come in contact.

He believes, for example, that scientific knowledge must be used to enable us to gain sufficient control over our environment to be able to get and maintain the things we value. This is a notion, however, which philosophers traditionally have been slow to accept, for two different but related reasons.

One reason has been the long-standing separation of actions into those that are morally relevant and those which are not. Thus Dewey says, "the narrow scope which moralists often give to morals, their isolation of some conduct as virtuous and vicious from other large ranges of conduct, those having to do with health and vigor, business, education, with all the affairs in which desires and affection are implicated, is perpetuated by this habit of exclusion of the subject-matter of natural science from a role in formation of moral standards and ideals."[40] For Dewey, the distinction between moral and nonmoral is a relative matter. He claims that "every act has *potential* moral significance, because it is, through its consequences, part of a larger whole of behavior."[41] Thus in Dewey's view, an act seen in isolation from its consequences may seem to have a nonmoral character just because it *is* seen in isolation. Once it is placed in its proper context and we are able to see the consequences of this act and compare them in imagination with probable consequences of alternate acts, we recognize the possibility of judging better or worse with respect to the actions before us and thereby introduce moral considerations.

The second reason for neglecting the importance of scientific knowledge for ethics has to do with traditional notions concerning goodness and values in general. Dewey points out that the weight of the greatest authorities for the past two thousand years has been on the side of believing in "the antecedent immutable reality of truth, beauty and goodness."[42] A belief which holds values to be a part of the real or of Being itself, is one which stands in the way of bringing to bear on values the positive results of science. In general, this situation has given rise to what Dewey calls "the crisis in contemporary culture."[43] This crisis and "the confusions and conflicts in it, arise," according to Dewey, "from a division of authority. Scientific inquiry seems to tell one thing, and traditional beliefs about ends and ideals that have authority over conduct tell us something quite different."[44] Further, Dewey says, "as long as the notion persists that values are authentic and valid only on condition that they are properties of Being independent of human action, as long as it is supposed that their right to regulate action is dependent upon their being independent of action, so long there will be needed schemes to prove that values are, in spite of the findings of science, genuine and known qualifications of reality in it-self."[44]

In *The Quest for Certainty*, Dewey points out how the need for and acceptance of authority and dogma in the realm of values is at least in part the result of the separation of theory from practicality, and knowledge from action. The irony of such a separation, as he notes, is that, while what people fundamentally desire is practical security (the ability to control conditions of the environment), they traditionally have settled for a less effective security. This is the security of ideas which is achieved by disconnecting knowledge from action and theory from practice.[46] In its turn, however, the reliance on dogma and authority in matters of value has stood in the way of further inquiry which would produce the practical security which was originally desired. Thus as Dewey points out:

> Just as belief that a magical ceremony will regulate the growth of seeds to full harvest stifles the tendency to investigate natural causes and their workings, so acceptance of dogmatic rules as bases of conduct in education, morals and social matters, lessens the impetus to find out about the conditions which are involved in forming intelligent plans.[47]

A second manner in which science and ethics interact, for Dewey, is through the use of ethics to guide the course of scientific inquiry. In the process of basing our moral judgments on the best scientific evidence available, we tend (by implication at least) to encourage scientific inquiry in some directions and discourage it in others. In particular, science is constantly under pressure to produce in areas and in ways which will improve the quality of life. As Dewey points out:

> Men desired heat, light, and speed of transit and of communication beyond what nature provides of itself. These things have been attained not by lauding the enjoyment of these things and preaching their desirability, but by study of the conditions of their manifestation.[48]

Consequently, Dewey states, "moral science is not something with a separate province. It is physical, biological and historic knowledge placed in a human context where it will illuminate and guide the activities of men."[49]

A third manner in which science and ethics impinge on one another concerns the opening of doors for ethics by scientific investigation. Prominent examples of this process can be found in current questions in bioethics and medical ethics. As the branches of science which deal with the prolongation and/or production of life become more sophisticated, questions arise for ethics which could never have arisen before. The situation has two sides, however. On the one hand, were science not to have progressed in these directions, we might have been spared the trouble of new areas of moral decision; on the other hand, the fact that there are new choices to be made means that new possibilities have opened up. Without such possibilities the hope for improving the quality of life is cut off. On this point Dewey says:

> Every gain in natural science makes possible new aims. That is, the discovery of how things *do* occur makes it possible to conceive of their happening at will, and gives us a start on selecting and combining the conditions, the means, to command their happening.[50]

Finally, Dewey describes a fourth manner in which ethics and science relate to one another. This last feature has to do with method. It is Dewey's proposal that ethics make use of the methods and techniques which have made progress in science possible.[51] Of primary importance in using the methods termed scientific is understanding how science works and what it tries to do. Dewey conceives of science as being concerned ultimately with acquiring the means to effect changes in the environment. To do so, however, involves a shift in how we deal with the world, from a superficial common sense level, to an underlying inferred level; that is, science does not deal with phenomena on their face value, but attempts to find out what operations which we can perform, describe, and repeat, will in fact effect a given result.[52] According to Dewey,

> what science actually does is to show that any natural object we please may be treated in terms of relations upon which its occurrence depends, or as an event, and that by so treating it we are enabled to get behind, as it were, the immediate qualities the object of direct experience presents, and to regulate their happening, instead of having to wait for conditions beyond our control to bring it about. Reduction of experienced objects to the form of relations, which are neutral as respects qualitative traits, is a prerequisite of ability to regulate the course of change, so that it may terminate in the occurrence of an object having desired qualities.[53]

And again:

> Thus the scientific conception carries thought and action away from qualities which are finalities as they are found in direct perception and use, to the mode of production of these qualities, and it performs this task in a way which links this mode of generation to a multitude of other "efficient" causal conditions in the most economical and effective manner.[54]

It is clear from these statements that if ethics is to become scientific, which is Dewey's desire, it too must cease its concern with features of human conduct which present themselves as qualitative finalities, such as presumably do feeling and intuitions. What is needed is to discover a level of dealing with human behavior which gives rise to fruitful regulation. That is to say, in order to make ethics effective, it must find a ground from which to operate. The ground must be one where experimental evidence may be presented showing that certain specifiable and repeatable conditions may be presented which will predictably produce certain results on a regular basis. In summarizing the required procedure, Dewey says:

> The first effect of experimental analysis is ... to reduce
> objects directly experienced to data. This resolution is
> required because the objects in their first mode of
> experience are perplexing, obscure, fragmentary; ...
> Given data which locate the nature of the problem, there
> is evoked a thought of an operation which if put into
> execution may eventuate in a situation in which the
> trouble or doubt which evoked inquiry will be re-
> solved.[55]

It should be noted that Dewey's suggestion, that if we are concerned ultimately with control of human conduct, we must shift from an introspective psychology of immediate qualities of experience to one which deals with aspects of human behavior experimentally demonstrated to be linked in certain predictable ways with certain other forms of behavior, is fundamentally a behavioristic notion. If we attempt to deal with ethical concepts which are founded upon the traditional introspective psychologies of the past, we are, according to Dewey, bound to be ineffectual. As he points out in *Human Nature and Conduct,* "the belief that we can know ourselves immediately is as disastrous to moral science as the corresponding idea regarding knowledge of nature was to physical science."[56]

In the case of human psychology, Dewey stresses the need for getting beyond immediate appearances and felt qualities to factors of behavior amenable to quantitative description and control. Specifically, we must deal with recurrences of behavior under generally specifiable conditions (habits, dispositions) and the conditions productive of these recurrences (impulses and factors of reinforcement). Hence,

> when correlations of changes are made the goal of
> knowledge, the fulfillment of its aim in discovery of
> these correlations, is equivalent to placing in our hands
> an instrument of control. When one change is given, and
> we know with measured accuracy its connection with
> another change, we have the potential means of produc-
> ing or averting that other event.[57]

According to Dewey, to say that we must use the methods of science in ethics and look beyond obvious qualitative features of human psychology to the measurable quantitative correlations of changes, however, is not to say that all matters of psychology relevant to ethics can be reduced to physical changes. Dewey is not a proponent of a simplistic form of behaviorism. A limitation, therefore, must be placed on the above discussion of scientific method in ethics. It involves the fact that, for Dewey, in knowledge of human affairs,

> we cannot indulge in the selective abstractions that are the secret of the success of physical knowing. When we introduce a like simplification into social and moral subjects we eliminate the distinctively human factors— reduction to the physical ensues.[58]

The discussion in this chapter has presented a synopsis of Dewey's views regarding the relation of ethics to science. The end of the discussion, however, has narrowed the topic to the relation of ethics to one particular science—psychology. This topic will be dealt with in greater detail in the following chapters.

Endnotes

[1] John Dewey, *Logic: The Theory of Inquiry* (New York: Henry Holt and Company, 1938), p. 105. See also, John Dewey, *Experience and Nature*, 2nd ed. (New York: W.W. Norton and Company, 1929; reprint ed., New York: Dover Publications, Inc., 1958), pp. 53-54.

[2] Dewey, *Logic*, p. 107.

[3] John Dewey, *Reconstruction in Philosophy* (New York: Henry Holt and Company, 1920; reprint ed., Boston: The Beacon Press, enlarged edition with new introduction, 1948), p. 161. See also, John Dewey, *The Influence of Darwin on Philosophy and Other Essays in Contemporary Thought* (New York: Henry Holt and Company, 1910), p. 48.

[4] John Dewey, *The Quest for Certainty* (New York: Minton, Balch and Company, 1929), Chapter Two.

[5] Ibid., p. 35.

[6] Ibid., p. 281.

[7] Dewey, *Reconstruction in Philosophy*, p. 161.

[8] Ibid., p. 172. Also see, Dewey, *The Quest for Certainty*, p. 274.

[9] Dewey, *The Quest for Certainty*, p. 270. See also, Dewey, *Experience and Nature*, pp. 53-4.

[10] Dewey, *Experience and Nature*. Also see John Dewey, "Experience, Knowledge and Value: A Rejoinder," in *The Philosophy of John Dewey*, edited by Paul Arthur Schilpp (LaSalle, Illinois: The Open Court Publishing Company, second edition, 1951; first published, 1939), p. 524.

[11] Dewey, *Reconstruction in Philosophy*, pp. 165-6.

[12] John Dewey, "The Field of 'Value'" in *Value: A Cooperative Inquiry*, edited by Ray Lepley (New York: Columbia University Press, 1949), p. 72. See also, John Dewey, *Human Nature and Conduct* (Modern Library edition, 1930; first published, New York: Henry Holt and Company, 1922), p. 12.

[13] John Dewey and James H. Tufts, *Ethics* (second edition revised; New York: Henry Holt and Company, 1932), p. 4.

[14] See Dewey, *Human Nature and Conduct*, p. 295, and Dewey, "Experience, Knowledge and Value: A Rejoinder," p. 554.

[15] Dewey, *Reconstruction in Philosophy*, p. 164.

[16] Dewey, *Human Nature and Conduct*, p. 181. See also, John Dewey, *The Problems of Men* (New York: Philosophical Library, 1946), p. 239; first published in *Studies in Logical Theory*, The University of Chicago Press, 1903.

[17] B. F. Skinner, *About Behaviorism* (New York: Alfred A. Knopf, Inc., 1974), p. 14.

[18] Dewey, *The Problems of Men*, p. 308.

[19] Dewey, *Reconstruction in Philosophy*, p. 84. Dewey's statement continues as follows:

> According to this theory, mental life originated in sensations which are separately and passively received, and which are formed, through laws of retention and association, into a mosaic of images, perceptions and conceptions. The senses were regarded as gateways or avenues of knowledge. Volition, action, emotion and desire follow in the wake of sensations and images. The intellectual or cognitive factor comes first and emotional and volitional life is only a consequent conjunction of ideas with sensations of pleasure and pain. The effect of the development of biology has been to reverse the

picture. Whenever there is life, there is behavior, activity. In order that life may persist, this activity has to be both continuous and adapted to the environment. This adaptive adjustment moreover, is not wholly passive; it is not a mere matter of the moulding of the organism by the environment.

[20] George Herbert Mead, *Mind Self and Society* (Chicago: University of Chicago Press, 1934), p. 2.

[21] Skinner, *About Behaviorism,* p. 16.

[22] Ibid., p. 3.

[23] Thus, Dewey says,

its meaning in terms of the great human uses to which it may be put, its meaning in the service of possibilities of secure value, offer a field for exploration which cries out from very emptiness. ....Philosophy under such conditions finds itself in no opposition to science. It is a liaison officer between the conclusions of science and the modes of social and personal action through which attainable possibilities are projected and striven for *(Quest for Certainty,* p. 311).

Also, he says,

here, then, lies the reconstruction work to be done by philosophy. It must undertake to do for the development of inquiry into human affairs and hence into morals what the philosophers of the last few centuries did for promotion of scientific inquiry in psychological conditions and aspects of human life (*Reconstruction in Philosophy,* p. xxiii).

And again, Dewey states, "thus is created the standing problem of modern philosophy: — the relation of science to the things we prize and love and which have authority in the direction of conduct" *(Quest for Certainty,* p. 103).

[24] Dewey, *The Quest for Certainty,* pp. 18-19.

[25] John Dewey, "Ethics and Physical Science," *Andover Review* 7 (June 1887); reprinted in *The Early Works of John Dewey,* 1882-1898, George E. Axtelle, et. al., eds., 5 vols. (Carbondale and Edwardsville: Southern Illinois University Press, 1969), 1:209.

[26] Ibid., p. 208.

[27] Ibid.

[28] Ibid., p. 209.

[29] Ibid., p. 210.

[30] Ibid., p. 214.

[31] Ibid., p. 216.

[32] Ibid., p. 217.

[33] Dewey, *Logic: The Theory of Inquiry,* p. 166.

[34] Dewey, "Ethics and Physical Science," p. 219.

[35] Ibid., p. 223.

[36] Ibid., pp. 218-219.

[37] Dewey, *The Quest for Certainty,* p. 260.

[38] Dewey, "Ethics and Physical Science," p. 220.

[39] Dewey and Tufts, *Ethics* (1932), pp. 6-7.

[40] Dewey, *The Quest For Certainty*, p. 274. Dewey further says:

> For moralists usually draw a sharp line between the field of the natural sciences and the conduct that is regarded as moral. But a moral that frames its judgments of value on the basis of consequences must depend in a most intimate manner upon the conclusions of science. For the knowledge of the relations between changes which enable us to connect things as antecedents and consequences *is* science (*The Quest for Certainty*, p. 274).

[41] Dewey and Tufts, *Ethics* (1932), p. 179.

[42] Dewey, *The Quest for Certainty*, p. 43.

[43] Ibid., p. 43.

[44] Ibid., pp. 43-44.

[45] Ibid., p. 44. Dewey also says,

> all that is required in order to apprehend that scientific knowledge as a mode of active operation is a potential ally of the modes of action which sustain values in existence, is to surrender the traditional notion that knowledge is possession of the inner nature of things and is the only way in which they may be experienced as they 'really' are (*The Quest for Certainty*, p. 131).

[46] On this Dewey says:

> It would be possible to argue (and, I think, with much justice) that failure to make action central in the search for such security as is humanly possible is a survival of the impotency of men in those stages of civilization when he had few means of regulating and utilizing the conditions upon which the occurrence of consequences depend. As long as man was unable by means of the arts of practice to direct the course of events, it was natural for him to seek an emotional substitute; in the absence of actual certainty in the midst of a precarious and hazardous world, men cultivated all sorts of things that would give them the *feeling* of certainty. And it is possible that, when not carried to an illusory point, the cultivation of the feeling gave men courage and confidence and enabled him to carry the burdens of life more successfully. But one could hardly seriously contend that this fact, if it be such, is one upon which to found a reasoned philosophy (*The Quest for Certainty*, p. 33).

[47] Dewey, *The Quest for Certainty*, p. 40.

[48] Ibid., pp. 268-269.

[49] Dewey, *Human Nature and Conduct*, p. 296.

[50] Ibid., p. 235.

[51] On this Dewey says "we are only pleading for the adoption in moral reflection of the logic that has been proved to make for security, stringency and fertility in passing judgments upon physical phenomena" (*Reconstruction in Philosophy*, p. 165).

[52] Dewey says, "Modern science no longer tries to find some fixed form or essence behind each process of change. Rather, the experimental method tries to break down apparent fixities and to induce changes" (*Reconstruction in Philosophy*, p. 113). Also, Dewey says,

> When the practice of knowledge ceased to be dialectical and became experimental, knowing became preoccupied with changes and the test of knowledge became the ability to bring about certain changes. Knowing, for the experimental sciences, means a certain kind of intelligently conducted doing; it ceases to be contemplative and becomes in a true sense practical (*Reconstruction in Philosophy*, p. 121).

[53] Dewey, *The Quest For Certainty*, pp. 104-105.

[54] Ibid., pp. 158-159.

[55] Ibid., p. 123.

[56] Dewey, *Human Nature and Conduct*, p. 253.

[57] Dewey, *The Quest for Certainty*, pp. 100-101.

[58] Ibid., p. 216.

꙲

OUTLINES OF DEWEY'S PSYCHOLOGY

1. Purpose, Method, and Scope of Psychology

In 1917, Dewey wrote that social psychology was now developed to the point that physical science had passed three centuries before.[1] The fact that psychology was only three hundred years behind physical science rather than two thousand years was due to the introduction of methods other than the introspective method of psychological investigation. When Dewey made this assessment in 1917, experimental methods in psychology were commonplace, and the transition in thinking about psychology's methods and goals was tending toward the last stage in what can be characterized as a three stage development. The first stage had centered around the belief that the true subject matter of psychology is consciousness and that its proper method of investigation is introspection. The second stage involved retention of the belief that psychology is a study of consciousness, but a shift in method from the exclusive use of introspection to a mixed introspective-experimental method. The last stage of the early development of psychology was marked by the acceptance of behavior (rather than consciousness) as the subject matter of study and an expansion of the use of experimental methods.

This transition in its actual occurrence was by no means the clearly defined process here outlined; rather, it was a groping struggle away from a type of psychology which had very little to show for itself, considering its long history, to a psychological perspective promising achievement of the general goals of science, prediction and control. An examination of Dewey's writings on psychology reveals that Dewey himself underwent phases of this same struggle. In his 1887 work, *Psychology,* for example, Dewey held to the belief that consciousness is what psychology studies. There, he says, "since the facts with which psychology has to do are those of consciousness, the study of consciousness itself must be the main source of knowledge of the facts."[2] At this point Dewey was willing to concede that although consciousness was the subject matter of psychology, introspection was not the only method by which it could be studied.[3] While recognizing that physiology must have some place in the study of psychology, Dewey, in an 1884 essay, "The New Psychology," denied that "direct conclusions regarding the nature of mental activities or their causes can be drawn from the character of nervous structure or function...."[4] Although direct conclusions could not be drawn from physiology to matters of consciousness, Dewey did hold that indirectly, through the use of introspection and physiological experiments, the new methods could be of value. Introspection alone had the drawback of leading some psychologists to believe that they had discovered all there was to be known about human psychology.[5] However, Dewey thought that what was universal about normal human consciousness and its development could be established by a combination of introspective and experimental methods.[6]

According to Dewey, with the recognition that conclusions of introspective psychology must be compared and adjusted to the results and conclusions of biology and history and other sciences concerned with "the origin and development of the various spheres of man's activity,"[7] it could be seen, he thought, how ignorant we really are of psychological matters. He wrote: "We know that that life of man whose unfolding furnishes psychology its material is the most difficult and complicated subject which man can investigate."[8]

The early attempts to make psychology experimental rather than introspective, and to separate psychology from philosophy, were two aspects of the same situation. One result of this separation was, for Dewey, the need to restate the relation of psychology to philosophy. If psychology was no longer merely to be a branch of philosophy, but rather to stand on its own, how was this to be reconciled with its former close relationship to philosophy? Dewey's answer was given in the title of his 1886 article, "Psychology as Philosophic Method." According to Dewey, "the nature of all objects of philosophical inquiry is to be fixed by finding out what experience says about them. And Psychology is the scientific and systematic account of this experience."[9] For Dewey, however, this was not to be taken as an indication that there are certain facts about man that only psychology can reveal and that philosophy must wait upon these facts. On the contrary, Dewey says

> no such distinction [can be made] in the nature of man,
> as that in one aspect he is "part of the partial world," and

24

hence the subject of a purely natural science, psychology, and in another the conscious subject for which all exists, the subject of philosophy...."[10]

The correct way to understand the relation of philosophy to science, was as follows:

There is an absolute self-consciousness. The science of this is philosophy. This absolute self-consciousness manifests itself in the knowing and acting of individual men. The science of this manifestation, a phenomenology, is psychology. The distinction is no longer concerned with man's being itself; it is a distinction of treatment, of ways of looking at the same material.[11]

In his attempts to state the relationship between philosophy and psychology during the period 1884–1887, Dewey's metaphysical perspective was that of an objective idealist. The influence of the Hegelian mode of thinking is evidenced in Dewey's use of the term "absolute self-consciousness" in the above quotation. Even in this idealism, however, there is a foreshadowing of the requirement in his thinking which could most effectively be filled by a behavioristic psychology. This requirement was that human experience and history should not be explained as the interaction of individual autonomous and self-sufficient "minds," but rather that some means be used to account for the similarity and continuity of thought and action, especially within a given cultural setting. That this phenomenon could be accounted for by an objective idealism was true, although the account was not scientific. It was not a way which could lead to the prediction and control of the elements of resemblance inherent in "individual" thought and actions when viewed collectively.[12]

The changeover from an idealistic metaphysic to the hypothesis that the environment and its interactions with organisms can be used to account for similarities in behavior and thought (including reference to the effects of genetic endowments resulting from the evolutionary histories of species which allow individuals to learn from contingencies of the environment) was a gradual one, as Dewey pointed out in a brief autobiography, "From Absolutism to Experimentalism." Dewey put the period of the waning influence of Hegel on his own thought at roughly 1885-1900. He described this process as gradual and incomplete.[13]

The influences which helped bring about this transition have been described in detail by Dewey's biographers.[14] Dewey himself wrote that

William James's *Psychology,* published in 1890, was the single most important philosophic influence entering his thinking "to give it new direction and quality...."[15] This one book, according to Dewey, "worked its way more and more into my ideas and acted as a ferment to transform old beliefs."[16]

After this initial transition (containing the apparent continuity noted above) Dewey's psychological views tended to stabilize, or change only in points of emphasis, throughout the remainder of his writing career. One reason for this, as Dewey points out, is that pragmatism itself has certain basic foundations. One of these is a behavioristic view of psychology. Dewey states in a work published in 1930 that:

> The psychological tendencies which have exerted an influence on instrumentalism are of a biological rather than a physiological nature. They are, more or less, closely related to the important movement whose promoter in psychology has been Doctor John Watson and to which he has given the name of Behaviorism. Briefly, the point of departure of this theory is the conception of the brain as an organ for the coordination of sense stimuli (to which one should add modifications caused by habit, unconscious memory, or what are called today "conditioned reflexes") for the purpose of effecting appropriate motor responses.[17]

From his early view of psychology as "the science of the reproduction of some universal content or existence, whether of knowledge or of action, in the form of individual, unsharable consciousness,"[18] Dewey came to believe that psychology must concern itself with human behavior in its social context and in terms of its development in that context. As a result, his earlier view (that individual psychology can be an effective part of psychology in general) was abandoned. Also abandoned was the use of the introspective method of investigation. The problem of the proper method to use in psychological investigation for Dewey was not caused by the introspective method's failure to give information, but rather because introspection alone does not make clear the nature of the information which it presents. Introspection at best gives only the end product of a person's development to that point, and not a guide or record of the actual development. To understand psychological development means to understand a person's behavior as it has been affected by his/her social environment. Thus, according to Dewey, even if introspection were "a

26

valid method in individual psychology, so called, it could not be of use in the investigation of social facts, even though those facts be labeled social mind or consciousness."[19] And even in the area of individual psychology, Dewey held out little chance of introspection giving useful information, since to have a true object of study for introspective (rather than social) psychology one would need an individual who was totally unsocialized—raised purely by and through the physical environment. Hence, Dewey points out that, although

> theoretically it is possible that the reorganization of native activities which constitute mind may occur through their exercise within a purely physical medium.... The sort of mind capable of development through the operation of native endowment in a nonsocial environment is on the moron order, and is practically, if not theoretically, negligible.[20]

Thus psychology became almost synonymous with social psychology for Dewey. "From the point of view of the psychology of behavior," according to Dewey, "all psychology is either biological or social psychology. And if it still be true that man is not only an animal but a social animal, the two cannot be dissevered when we deal with man."[21] The task of social psychology, as Dewey saw it, involves describing the behavioral changes which take place when environmental conditions are altered. The resulting observable changes in behavior may then be directed or controlled through controlling the environment. Eventually, such information may be used to help restructure social institutions.[22]

Put negatively, it can be said that for Dewey, the problem for psychology was no longer that of explaining the relationship of a "mythical psychology of a mass or crowd or public mind, but as the problem of the relationship of original native activities to acquired capacities and habits."[23]

In summary, then, if psychology were to become scientific, according to Dewey, it must seek explanations for individual behavior in the social environment. At the same time it must not attempt to account for the social environment by reference to the idealistic metaphysics presupposed in the concept of "social mind." A scientific psychology must also change its method from introspection to a method more suited to its new task. Accordingly, the new method which would replace introspection for Dewey must be one capable of dealing with individuals in terms of their development, especially their social dimensions. The method must further be able to afford the science of psychology a basis for experimentation, prediction, and control—something the introspective method was unable to do. An additional characteristic of any scientific treatment of psychology was that it must be pluralistic, and not attempt to reduce all psychological phenomena to one principle. Furthermore, it must suppose "the complexity and specific variety of the factors of human nature, each operating in response to its own stimulus, and each subject to almost infinite shadings and modifications as it enters into combinations and competition with others."[24] Finally, the method in question must be one which does not begin from the position taken by "the traditional psychology" which postulates an "original separate soul, mind or consciousness...."[25] The result of such a postulate is to "cut human nature off from its natural objective relations. It implies first the severance of man from nature and then of each man from his fellows."[26]

The method of psychological investigation which could fulfill all of these needs for Dewey was behaviorism. The introduction of behaviorism into psychology was the boost needed to bring about meaningful experimentation in other than the physiological realm of psychology. The place of method in inquiry was all important for Dewey and "the introduction of experimental method [in psychology] is all one with interest in control— in *modification* of the future."[27] Behaviorism as a method was important for Dewey because "it represents not an improvement in detail but a different mode of attack."[28] This is the case because

> it [behaviorism] transfers attention from vague generalities regarding social consciousness and social mind to the specific processes of interaction which take place among human beings, and to the details of group-behavior. It emphasizes the importance of knowledge of the primary activities of human nature, and of the modifications and reorganizations they undergo in association with the activities of others. It radically simplifies the whole problem by making it clear that social institutions and arrangements, including the whole apparatus of tradition and transmission, represent simply the acquired transformation of original human endowments.[29]

2. Origins of Dewey's Behaviorism

Early behavioristic psychology was grounded in an attempt to explain all aspects of human behavior through a "reflex arc," a stimulus and response. While still seeking a unifying principle for his psychological views, Dewey briefly made use of the reflex arc concept in his own teaching.[30] In 1896, however, he wrote "The Reflex Arc Concept in Psychology" in which he was highly critical of this principle, although he admitted that it "has upon the whole come nearer to meeting the demand for a general working hypothesis than any other single concept."[31] In the process of his criticism, Dewey set forth some of the leading views of his later developed behavioristic psychology.

As its explanatory apparatus, the reflex arc concept makes use of the terms 'stimulus' and 'response.' While these terms are potentially helpful instrumentalities for guiding thought, in actual practice, Dewey found the terms being used by some psychologists as if they referred to distinct and separable parts of experience. This is an example of a fallacy Dewey often called attention to: the fallacy of reading into experience (as an antecedent condition) a distinction which was the result of an inquiry into experience.[32] For Dewey, any attempt to separate stimulus from a response was an artificial abstraction from experience and did not reflect the true nature of the case. When one leaves the world of abstractions and examines the situation on its own terms, a stimulus is found to be a stimulus only under certain conditions; the same is true of a response. Food may serve as a stimulus to someone who is hungry, but not to someone with the stomach flu. Before an organism can respond to a stimulus it must be "ready"; that is, the state of an organism prior to a potential stimulation will determine whether the organism is to respond at all, and, if so, in what way.[33] In addition, Dewey believed that the stimulus and response must be seen as a circuit allowing for a transfer of information in both directions.[34] For example, "the ability of the hand to do its work," according to Dewey, "will depend, either directly or indirectly, upon its control, as well as its stimulation, by the act of vision."[35]

In terms of his developing behavioristic psychology, the conception of stimulus and response as a circuit helped explain and further develop his idea of impulse "mediation," as developed in *The Study of Ethics: A Syllabus*.[36] "Mediation" is how Dewey labels the fact that in the stimulus-response relation there is a back-reference of the stimulus to past responses.[37] Once someone has responded to a light by reaching for it, touching it, and being burned, the next seeing of a light will be a "seeing-of-a-light-that-means-pain-when-contact-occurs."[38] This way of conceptualizing the matter makes the organism itself an ongoing developing agency, and its acts, not individual, isolated occurrences, but biographical clues to the organism's past interactions with its environment. This, as will be shown in Chapter Four, is the core of B. F. Skinner's view of reinforcement—a concept which plays a central role in his behaviorism.

In his criticism of the reflex arc concept, Dewey also notes that it contains an implicit assumption of mind-body duality. Thus he states: "The older dualism of body and soul finds a distinct echo in the current dualism of stimulus and response."[39] As will be elaborated below in the discussion of Dewey's view of the mind, the rejection of mind-body dualism held a central position in Dewey's developed psychology. What have been referred to as mind and body (as separate entities) on Dewey's analysis turn out to be only different aspects of organic activity in its interaction with the environment.[40] Within the same article Dewey used the biological evolution of the species as an explanatory tool to account for present behavioral phenomena. In his discussion of stimuli, for example, Dewey argued that it is for reasons of evolutionary background that one sense organ cannot be stimulated at the expense of others. Since the "ear activity has been evolved on account of the advantage gained by the whole organism," according to Dewey, "it must stand in strictest histological and physiological connection with the eye, or hand, or leg, or whatever other organ has been the overt centre of action."[41]

Finally, Dewey's essay "The Reflex Arc Concept in Psychology" takes a behavioristic stand toward sensation. There is not, for Dewey, a stimulus as an external and observable phenomenon in addition to a response which is an internal and, in principle, unobservable phenomenon. Rather, there is one event when a sound is heard, for example, and that is the act of hearing.[42] Thus "it is just as true to say," according to Dewey, "that the sensation of sound arises from a motor response as that the running away is a response to the sound."[43]

It is significant that in this early article Dewey anticipated or explicitly advanced many of the elements of his later fully developed behavioristic psychology. Also, in accordance with the general definition of behaviorism presented in Chapter One, it is noteworthy that Dewey was by this time primarily a behaviorist in his orientation toward psychology.

3. Organism and Environment

The generic context of explanation for the psychological theory which was to be accepted by Dewey throughout most of his writing career was the model of an organism and its interactions with its environment not as separate and distinct parcels of experience, but in mutual transaction. This context formed the basis for all further aspects of his psychological theory. Hence Dewey says: "Whatever else organic life is or is not, it is a process of activity that involves an environment. It is a transaction extending beyond the spatial limits of the organism. An organism does not live *in* an environment; it lives by means of an environment."[44]

The term "environment" is used by Dewey in what might be described as a relative sense. That is, he does not speak of the environment as if there were something absolute over and above the conditions involved in life. And even when considering the environment purely in terms of conditions of life, distinctions must be made with respect to those conditions necessary for some forms of life as distinct from those necessary for others. The environment of a carrot, for example, is not the same environment in which a sparrow lives, although the environment of each is determined in the same way. Thus in an unavoidably "question begging way," Dewey says: "In brief, the environment consists of those conditions that promote or hinder, stimulate or inhibit, the *characteristic* activities of a living being."[45] Or, conversely he says: "There are things in the world that are indifferent to the life-activities of an organism. But they are not parts of *its* environment, save potentially."[46]

The above statement, although taken to characterize organic life generally, applies to human life as well. Hence, Dewey says "the things with which a man *varies* are his genuine environment."[47] In the case of human life, more so than in the case of other forms of life, a primary part is played by social aspects of the environment. Our activities are certainly varied in response to other people's activities and responses, and thus (by definition) those other people form an aspect of our environment. "The social environment" for Dewey, "consists of all the activities of fellow beings that are bound up in the carrying on of the activities of any one of its members."[48] Although Dewey's moral theory will not be discussed until the next chapter, it should be noted here that the most basic connection between moral life and psychology takes place in the context just described—the social environment. It is because we form part of one another's social environments that we are presented with problems called "moral."

Within the environment, the organism, as a living being, has certain characteristics which set it off from nonliving things. Thus Dewey says

> to live signifies that a connected continuity of acts is effected in which preceding ones prepare the conditions under which later ones occur. There is a chain of cause and effects, of course, in what happens with inanimate things. But for living creatures, the chain has a particular cumulative continuity, or else death ensues.[49]

When considered together, the organism and its environment form a potential unity. "The processes of living are enacted by the environment as truly as by the organism; for they *are* an integration."[50] The interactions between organism and environment have a goal, once it is presupposed that there is value in maintaining life. The goal is, according to Dewey, "to maintain the conditions in both of them needed for later interactions."[51] That is, a dynamic inertia or self-perpetuation of possibilities of further self-perpetuation forms the purpose or goal of the organism-environment interaction.

When the goal is not reached, the equilibrium of the organism and its environment is upset. The result is activity on the part of the organism to reestablish equilibrium. "Indeed," says Dewey, "living may be regarded as a continual rhythm of disequilibrations and recoveries of equilibrium."[52] Furthermore, "when the balance within a given activity [of an organism] is disturbed then there is exhibited need, search and fulfillment (or satisfaction) in the objective meaning of those terms."[53] In stressing that he is referring to the objective meaning of the terms involved, Dewey's point is that the activities in question can be described through observation. Dewey gives a behavioristic account of each term involved. When he speaks of need, for example, he is not referring to a feeling or mental state. "The state of disturbed equilibration constitutes need."[54] Similarly, Dewey says, "the movement towards [the organism's]...restoration is search and exploration."[55] And "the recovery [of equilibrium] is fulfillment or satisfaction."[56] The satisfaction is evidenced by the cessation of activity, not by a feeling, although a feeling may accompany the cessation of activity.

In the interaction between the organism and its environment, neither the organism nor the environment can be described as dominant. "The environment can at most," according to Dewey, "only supply stimuli to call out responses. These responses proceed from tendencies already possessed by the individual."[57] To refer to the relationship of the organism to its environment as a case of stimulus and response, however, is to oversimplify the situation. Some of the reasons for this were noted above in the discussion of Dewey's "The Reflex Arc Concept in Psychology." To more accurately describe how it is that the environment "calls out" a response in an organism, rather than mechanically evoking a response, Dewey describes two different "modes of environing-organical interactions to which the names excitation-reaction and stimulus-response may be applied."[58] When an organism responds to a change in its environment, but only to the extent of noting the change, Dewey calls this excitation-reaction. For example, when a person jumps but does nothing else when he hears a sudden noise, Dewey refers to this as "excitation-reaction."[59]

The primary characteristic of such an interaction is that "the excitation is specific and so is the reaction."[60]

When the organism is not merely noting a change in its environment, but is called into action because of the change, Dewey labels this "stimulus-response." His position with respect to what is meant by a stimulus and a response was quite consistent between "The Reflex Arc Concept in Psychology," and his 1938 *Logic: The Theory of Inquiry*. For this reason it will not be necessary to repeat the discussion of this mode of interaction. It should be noted that in differentiation from an excitation-reaction, a stimulus-response involves a coordinated and organized response on the part of the organism. The response involves deciphering aspects of the environment—that is, responding not to environmental elements as such, but responding to their *meanings*. Thus, stimulus-response reactions require previous experience and learning.[61]

4. Impulsion, Impulse, and Desire

When an interaction between an organism and its environment is not called out by the environment but is, rather, initiated by a tension or need within the organism itself, Dewey refers to this expressed need as an "impulsion." "Impulsions are the beginnings of complete experience," for Dewey, "because they proceed from need; from a hunger and demand that belongs to the organism as a whole and that can be supplied only by instituting definite relations (active relations, interactions) with the environment."[62]

At this point, it may be noted that there is a certain analogy between Dewey's concept of an impulsion and his concept of an excitation. Once an excitation becomes integrated with meaningful aspects of the environment it ceases to be merely an excitation and becomes part of the circuit of stimulus-response. Similarly, when an impulsion becomes connected with the aspects of the environment which can fulfill the need which it expresses, it ceases to be an impulsion and becomes an impulse. Thus Dewey says:

> Every experience, of slight or tremendous import, begins with an impulsion, rather *as* an impulsion. I say "impulsion" rather than "impulse." An impulse is specialized and particular; it is, even when instinctive, simply a part of the mechanism involved in a more complete adaptation with the environment. "Impulsion" designates a movement outward and forward of

the whole organism to which special impulses are auxiliary. It is the craving of the living creature for food as distinct from the reactions of tongue and lips that are involved in swallowing; the turning toward light of the body as a whole, like the heliotropism of plants, as distinct from the following of a particular light by the eyes.[63]

Common to both impulses and impulsions is the fact that they are blind with respect to the probable sources of fulfillment in the environment. For Dewey

impulsion from need starts an experience that does not know where it is going; resistance and check bring about the conversion of direct forward action into reflection; what is turned back upon is the relation of hindering conditions to what the self possesses as working capital in virtue of prior experiences.[64]

Impulses, then, are native activities which are more specialized than impulsions. As original or native activities of an organism impulses, according to Dewey, might also be called "instincts," although the latter term is more ambiguous. Thus, in *Human Nature and Conduct,* Dewey says:

The use of the words instinct and impulse as practical equivalents is intentional, even though it may grieve critical readers. The word instinct taken alone is still too laden with the older notion that an instinct is always definitely organized and adapted—which for the most part is just what it is not in human beings. The word impulse suggests something primitive, yet loose, undirected, initial. Man can progress as beasts cannot, precisely because he has so many "instincts" that they cut across one another, so that most serviceable actions must be *learned.*[65]

The difficulty with discussing behavior in terms of instincts is that they are often taken as explanations for behavior.[66] This occurs when instincts are taken as specialized structures in behavior, rather than as loose potentialities. Thus, what often happens, according to Dewey, is that the alleged instincts "appealed to as a causal force themselves represent physiological tendencies which have previously been shaped into habits of action and expectation by means of the very activities which they are supposed to explain."[67]

Instincts properly understood are not the kinds of entities which can be listed and catalogued. Hence, Dewey says: "In man, there are very few instincts pure and simple, but rather the loose beginnings and ends of very many instincts .... Hence also the impossibility of a systematic classification of fundamental impulses to action."[68] Because of these potential confusions concerning the meaning of the term 'instinct,' then, it is less misleading to use the term 'impulse' as Dewey himself more often does.

Impulses are important ingredients in Dewey's psychology since they form the basis for habits. Impulses are temporally prior to specific habits, to which they give rise, but they are never solidified into habits.[69] This is the case because for Dewey impulses are the "native or spontaneous way in which the self acts."[70] Furthermore, just as Dewey said that all experience begins as impulsion, he says that "all conduct is at first impulsive. It has no end *consciously* in view.... All activity is impulsive so far as containing new elements—so far, that is, as it is not purely habitual."[71]

That impulses do not become habits is further demonstrated by certain facts of organic life. One such fact is that organisms adjust to changes in their environments. If impulses were to become habits, there would be no basis for such adjustment. The need for an adjustment is brought about because the regular or habitual way in which an organism has discovered that it can fulfill a certain need is met with frustration. In such an instance the impulse which gave rise to the habit (through successful fulfillment of a need) is stymied and eventually released to seek new means of fulfillment. That this is the case is shown by the fact that specific impulses may find more than one mode of fulfillment. Thus, according to Dewey:

> Impulse does not know what it is after; it cannot give orders, not even if it wants to. It rushes blindly into any opening it chances to find. Anything that expends it, satisfies it. One outlet is like another to it.[72]

He further amplifies:

> In the case of the young it is patent that impulses are highly flexible starting points for activities which are diversified according to the ways in which they are used. Any impulse may become organized into almost

any disposition according to the way it interacts with surroundings.[73]

Thus, to summarize these points, it can be said that, for Dewey, an organism first expresses a need through an impulsion. When the expression becomes specific and localized it is an impulse seeking fulfillment. As an impulse, however, it may be fulfilled in various ways. When a particular way of fulfillment is regularly found effective, the organism specifically seeks out that form of fulfillment and can be said to have formed a habit.

This, however, is not the complete story. The process involved when an organism seeks fulfillment for its impulses and then either finds or fails to find such fulfillment is a process which molds and forms the organism. We learn from each experience, not in the sense of storing new memories about the past, but in the sense that we are actually transformed by our experience. This is the fact referred to above when Dewey spoke of having our impulses mediated. This is why, according to Dewey, *"the expression of every impulse stimulates other experiences and these react into the original impulse and modify it."*[74] Through the process of having our impulses modified or mediated by their stimulation of other impulses we gradually become increasingly aware of the full range of consequences which may follow upon attempts to fulfill our different impulses in various ways. And this, according to Dewey, forms the psychological basis of moral conduct.[75]

The fact that for Dewey, "each impulse in its expression tends to call up to other impulses"[76] is of fundamental importance in explaining human behavior. This is so because the degree to which an impulse calls up other impulses and the way in which the impulses in question relate to one another affects the ways in which a person is able to react to his/her environment. The acts which an individual perform which are impulsive in the sense of stemming from unmediated impulses are those likely to be least effective in gaining for us what we want from our environment. On the other hand, impulses which have been completely mediated and integrated with other impulses are what we call habits. Our habits represent (in their potential) our most effective ways of interacting with our environment. Between the two extremes of unmediated impulses and those so thoroughly mediated to be called habits is a continuum. Toward the center of this continuum are what can be called dispositions or increased tendencies to act in certain ways under certain conditions.[77] It is important, for Dewey, as mentioned above, that not all our actions have become habituated for then we would be unable to adjust to new situations. On the other hand, it is important that not all our actions spring from unmediated impulses as well, for in that case, as Dewey points out, "our whole time would be taken up with minute and anxious reflection and our deeds would have no effectiveness."[78]

The mediation of impulses can take place in two general ways. The mediation may be due to natural activities of the organism itself, or due to specific conditions of the environment. Thus, for Dewey,

> the mediation of the impulse through the experiences it excites, may be comparatively organic or comparatively external. That is, some "results" are almost entirely conditioned upon the relation of the impulse expressed to other organs of action—as satisfaction from food when hungry, burning hand from putting it in fire, etc., while others are due more to circumstances which accompany the act at the time, but which may be absent as a rule—as poison may be found in a food usually healthy.[79]

As noted above, impulses in their original form are blind in the sense that they do not know antecedently what it is which will fulfill them. However, once an impulse has been fulfilled, it is easy to neglect this fact and assume that the impulse reached its goal because of a *desire for that goal*. To characterize the situation in the latter way is, for Dewey, to read back into a situation as an antecedent condition what can only properly be said to exist ex post facto. A desire, according to Dewey, "adds nothing to impulse excepting *consciousness* of the impulse."[80] Restated, he says

> the development of desire is constituted by the progressive objectification of impulse.... Impulse becomes desire when it ceases to be a mere outgoing towards something which is not consciously presented to the mind, and becomes distinguished from the self as a possible end of action. Desire implies a consciousness which can distinguish between its actual state and a possible future state, and is aware of the means by which this future state can be brought into existence.[81]

In concrete terms this means for Dewey that:

> A child, led by impulse, has put a piece of sugar in his mouth, just as, under the same circumstances, he would put a piece of stone into his mouth. But his action results

in a state of pleasure wholly unforeseen by him. Now the next time the child sees the sugar he will not merely have the impulse to put it in his mouth. There will also be the remembrance of the pleasure enjoyed from the sugar previously. There is consciousness of sugar as satisfying impulse and hence desire for it.[82]

In his explanation of the relation between impulse and desire Dewey notes that an impulse carried through to fulfillment with no obstacle presented to it is not a desire.[83] A desire occurs rather when an impulse is blocked and we become aware that there is or has been something which in the past has fulfilled that impulse. A tension is present. Hence, "the end-in-view of desire" according to Dewey, "is that object which were it present would link into an organized whole activities which are now partial and competing."[84]

5. Habit, Character, and Conduct

As already mentioned, when an individual's responses and ways of behaving become so organized as not to need conscious reflection prior to action, we are said to have habits. As Dewey notes, "a habit is a form of executive skill, of efficiency in doing. A habit means an ability to use natural conditions as means to ends. It is an active control of the environment through control of the organs of action."[85] Further, he says "habits are the tools which put at our immediate disposal the results of our former experiences, thus economizing force...."[86] ("Bad habits" are discussed below on page 39)

Habits, for Dewey, however, are double-edged swords. We pay a price for the efficiency of action and ease of choice which they make possible. By forming habits we restrict the need for conscious consideration of what we are doing. As a result our thoughts are bounded by specific limits, and we may fail to consider all possibilities in a situation.[87]

In anticipation of the discussion of Dewey's ethics in Chapter Three it should be noted here that for Dewey the growth of an individual is marked by the degree to which he/she is able to strike a balance between the inefficiency wrought by insufficient habitual behavior, and the rigidity of responses which may result from overdeveloped habits.[88] This point will be important in considering the moral development of an individual.

Dewey clarifies his definition of habit by explaining that the extent of our habitual activity is not limited to those specific acts which we routinely perform in specific ways. A large portion of our behavior is potentially habitual, although it may not seem routine. This is made clear when Dewey specifies that a habit is an "acquired predisposition to *ways* or modes of response, not to particular acts except ... under, special conditions. ...Habit means special sensitiveness or accessibility to certain classes of stimuli, standing predilections and aversions, rather than a bare recurrence of specific acts."[89] Viewed from this perspective habits are adjustments we have made, and it is likely that we may not even be aware of a large percentage of them, though they are involved in our actions.[90] This is equally true of both our ways of thinking and our overt actions. Hence, Dewey says "the significance of habit is not exhausted, however, in its executive and motor phase. It means formation of intellectual and emotional disposition as well as an increase in ease, economy, and efficiency of action."[91]

One further pertinent point concerning habits is the fact that what habits an individual happens to acquire is to a large extent accidental. Thus, just as impulses may be fulfilled in different ways at different times, so the ways in which a person learns to adjust to his environment in general are the result of how his/her impulses have actually been fulfilled in his/her environment. Once we acquire certain habits, we have not merely "picked up" general ways of responding to given types of conditions, but have ourselves been changed by the habits which have become part of us. Accordingly, Dewey states that

> we are given to thinking of a habit as simply a recurrent external mode of action, like smoking or swearing, being neat or negligent in clothes and person, taking exercise, or playing games. But habit reaches even more significantly down into the very structure of the self; it signifies a building up and solidifying of certain desires; an increased sensitiveness and responsiveness to certain stimuli; a confirmed or an impaired capacity to attend to and think about certain things. Habit covers in other words the very make-up of desire, intent, choice, disposition which gives an act its voluntary quality.[92]

This is a significant point because it implies that habits we acquire at one time will have a direct bearing on what habits we will be likely to acquire at later points in our lives. This point is demonstrated with special strength in the consideration of "bad habits." "A bad habit," according to Dewey, "suggests an inherent tendency to action and also a hold, command over us. It makes us do things we are ashamed of, things which we tell ourselves we prefer not to do. It overrides our formal resolutions, our conscious decisions."[93]

If we generalize the case of bad habits to cover all habits, it becomes obvious that what we consider our good habits are under the control of our intellectual decisions only to the degree that our bad habits are. In a sense we are our habits regardless of what other picture we may have set before ourselves. Dewey summarizes the nature of habits and their relation to our "self" by pointing out that a habit is

> that kind of human activity which is influenced by prior activity and in that sense acquired; which contains within itself a certain...systematization of minor elements of action; which is projective and, dynamic in quality, ready for overt manifestation; and which is operative in some subdued...form even when not obviously dominating activity.[94]

When viewed in their interconnection with one another, habits can be seen as composing a whole. One habit influences another habit, some habits lead to other habits, and through this interconnectedness a person's habits can be said to form his/her character. For example, in *The Problems of Men* Dewey notes that

> not only through habit does a given mental attitude expand into a particular case, but every habit in its own operation may directly or indirectly call up any other habit. The term "character" denotes this complex continuum of interactions in its office of influencing final judgment.[95]

It should be noted that far from using the term "character" as an explanation for conduct, Dewey uses the concept of character as a derived notion. That is, Dewey does not say that our habits are caused by our character, but rather that what is meant by our character can only be understood in the light of an understanding of our habits. What habits we have (which make up our character) are, in turn, determined by our actual conduct. We cannot have habits apart from their manifestation in our conduct. For example, it would not be meaningful to say that "I have the habit of sleeping late although I never use this habit since I always get up early." For Dewey, the interpretation of habit as well as character is based on conduct and is thus behavioristic. In making this point Dewey says "character...has no reality apart from the acts in which [mediated] impulses must sooner or later issue."[96]

The terms 'habit,' 'character,' and 'conduct' are all interrelated for Dewey. 'Conduct' refers to an individual's behavior seen not as a series of individual and isolated acts, but rather as a unity. Dewey says "the word [conduct] expresses continuity of action.... Where there is conduct there is not simply a succession of disconnected acts but each thing done carries forward an underlying tendency and intent, *conducting*, leading up, to further acts and to final fulfillment or consummation."[97] In addition,

> if an act were connected with other acts merely in the way in which the flame of a match is connected with an explosion of gun powder, there would be action, but not conduct. But our actions not only lead up to other actions which follow as their effects but they also leave an enduring impress on the one who performs them, strengthening and weakening permanent tendencies to act. This fact is familiar to us in the existence of *habit*.[98]

From these remarks, it can be understood that it is not in any casual way that conduct and character are related through habit. The continuity needed to transform behavior from mere action to conduct is brought about through the mediating of impulses and finally through the production of habits. These, in turn, when seen together, are a person's character. In clarifying this point further Dewey says

> acts are not linked up together to form conduct in and of themselves, but because of their common relation to an enduring and single condition—the self or character as the abiding unity in which different acts leave their lasting traces.[99]

Of the concept of character, Dewey notes that no one is ever a completed or finished character. Since habits may always change and impulses may be mediated in new ways, there is always room for change and growth.[100] Character is thus a tentative concept, something we attribute to someone after the fact, not as a cause or explanation of conduct.

Dewey summarizes these remarks about conduct, habit, and character by saying that "conduct and character are strictly correlative. Continuity, consistency, throughout a series of acts is the expression of the enduring unity of attitudes and habits. Deeds hang together because they proceed from a single and stable self."[101]

Dewey's reference to a "single and stable self" should not be construed to imply that there exists for him a metaphysical self, as cause and explanation, which lies behind an individual's actions. On the nature of self, Dewey states: "Every living self causes acts and is itself caused in return by what it does. All voluntary action is a remaking of self, since it creates new desires, instigates to new modes of endeavor, brings to light new conditions which institute new ends."[109]

The self for Dewey is not the same as the character, but not because the self is more real or more involved in the production of actions, but rather because the character is essentially a normative concept. He talks about character in the context of moral situations, but it is merely a shorthand way of referring to the self with a certain emphasis. Clarifying the nature of self further, Dewey notes that

> there is no one ready-made self behind activities. There are complex, unstable, opposing attitudes, habits, impulses which gradually come to terms with one another, and assume a certain consistency of configuration, even though only by means of a distribution of inconsistencies which keeps them in water-tight compartments, giving them separate turns or tricks in action.[103]

6. Motives, Emotions, and Feelings

The concept of motives is, according to Dewey, "extra-psychological."[104] "It is," he says, "an outcome of the attempt of men to influence human action...."[105] In desiring to control behavior, it is natural to look for events which can be related to other events as causes and effects. Traditionally, a motive was supposed to be just such an explanation. Once the explanation is known, the individual can be "caused" to do what is desired by appealing to the appropriate motive. Hence, according to the traditional view, if a correlation is established between getting a person to act as we want by the offering of money, for example, it can be said that money is a motive.

What is mistaken about the traditional or common sense view of motives is that it misrepresents the status of motives. This is true in one sense when it is assumed that to know someone's motive in a certain situation is to explain the situation. For Dewey, however, to determine what the motive is in a certain situation is to give no new information about that situation.[106] In another sense, the traditional view of motives misconstrues the nature of motives by taking them to be inducements "which operate from without upon the self."[107] The latter view, according to Dewey, confuses motives with stimuli.

What is responsible in part for the traditional confusion concerning the nature of motives is the fact that the term 'motive' is ambiguous. In common-sense thought one of the meanings of 'motive' is taken to be *the* meaning to the exclusion of all others. This results in artificially dividing a unity and thereby falsifying the nature of motives. The ambiguity of the term 'motive' lies in the fact that it sometimes means "those *interests* which form the core of the self and supply the principles by which conduct is to be understood," while at other times it "signifies the *object,* whether perceived or thought of, which effect an alteration in the direction of activity."[108]

For Dewey a motive is not an agency housed within the individual. The concept of motive, according to Dewey, must be understood as a relation of the individual's environment to his/her character—that is, it must be understood in the relation of the two meanings of the ambiguous term 'motive.' Thus Dewey says that a motive "is but an abbreviated name for the attitude and predisposition toward ends which is embodied in action...."[109]

When the habits and dispositions which make up character are seen as having goals, a motive is what brings the actions which lead to the desired goal. Thus Dewey points out: "Motive is only character in a given instance. Motive is never a bare natural impulse, but is impulse in the light of the consequences which may reasonably be supposed to result from acting upon it."[110] Thus a motive is not a goal external to the individual, as when a person is said to be motivated by money, nor a purely internal state, as when a person is said to be motivated by the feeling of rage. Motivation to action involves the whole of which the goal, character, and impulses (which have been mediated into dispositions) are only parts. This is the case since there must be something within the individual which can respond, and a desire or goal which the response is directed toward. Dewey summarizes these points in *Human Nature and Conduct* when he says

> a motive is then that element in the total complex of a man's activity which, if it can be sufficiently stimulated, will result in an act having specified consequences. And part of the process of intensifying (or reducing) certain elements in the total activity and thus regulating actual consequences is to impute these elements to a person as his actuating motives.[111]

And he summarizes their behavioristic implications in the 1932 *Ethics* when he says:

> A motive is not then a drive *to* action, or something which moves *to* doing something. It *is* the movement of the self as a whole, a movement in which desire is integrated with an object so completely as to be chosen as a compelling end. The hungry person seeks food. We may say, if we please, that he is moved by hunger. But in fact hunger is only a name for the tendency to move toward the appropriation of food. To create an entity out of this active relation of the self to objects, and then to treat this abstraction as if it were the cause of seeking food is sheer confusion. The case is no different when we say that a man is moved by kindness, or mercy, or cruelty, or malice. These things are not independent powers which stir to action. They are designations of the kind of active union or integration which exists between the self and a class of objects. It is the man himself in his very self who is malicious or kindly, and these adjectives signify that the self is so constituted as to act in certain ways towards certain objects. Benevolence or cruelty is not something which a man *has,* as he may have dollars in his pocketbook; it is something which he *is;* and since his being is active, these qualities are *modes of activity,* not forces which produce action.[112]

The concept of motive is further clarified by pointing out what is not a constituent of its definition. Hence, as Dewey points out, a motive is *not* something which exists prior to an act and which produces that act. Rather, "it is an act plus a judgment upon some element of it, the judgment being made in the light of the consequences of the act."[113] Further, a motive is not a feeling, "but the set disposition, of which a feeling is at best but a dubious indication."[114]

Dewey specifies the nature of feelings by pointing out that

> "feeling" is in general a name for the newly actualized quality acquired by events previously occurring upon a physical level, when these events come into more extensive and delicate relationships of interaction. More

specifically, it is a name for the coming to existence of those ultimate differences in affairs which mark them off from one another and give them discreteness .... [115]

Feelings, according to Dewey, are not to be identified with motives.[116] In contrast to feelings, however, emotions (interpreted behavioristically) may be seen as motives. Thus Dewey says "an emotion, as the word suggests, moves us, but emotion is a good deal more than a bare 'feeling'; anger is not so much a state of conscious feeling as it is a tendency to act in a destructive way towards whatever arouses it."[117] Specifically, an emotion for Dewey is "a perturbation from clash or failure of habit."[118]

Finally, a motive is not, as sometimes held, different from a person's intent. Accordingly, Dewey says, "the distinction between motive and intent is not found in the facts themselves, but simply a result of our own analysis, according as we emphasize either the emotional or the intellectual aspects of an action."[119] When the emotion which was aroused by the desire for a goal is emphasized in a situation *it* is seen as a motive. However, when in the same situation, the goal which called forth the emotion is seen as the point of emphasis, *it* is called the motive. In fact, both are integral parts of the same situation.

7. Mind, Consciousness, and Intelligence

It was Dewey's contention that a conceptual difference could be maintained between mind and consciousness, and that, although conceptually they were two things, they are so closely related that one cannot be adequately understood without reference to the other. To understand Dewey's conception of mind it is first necessary to understand his view of knowing—at least in rough outline. His view of knowing, however, is closely connected with his concept of meaning, and this concept itself is only fully understood when seen in the context in which meaning initially arises: the organism's interactions with its environment. Dewey's general position with respect to what happens when an organism interacts with its environment has been set out above. The major conceptual tools Dewey used to make the contents of that interaction clear were impulsion, impulse, mediation of impulse, and habit. As noted in the earlier discussion of these concepts, when an impulse becomes mediated, certain aspects of the individual's environment take on meaning. Only when aspects of the environment take on meaning through an organism's interaction with them can those aspects properly be said to be known.[120]

In *The Quest for Certainty* Dewey describes the process of knowing as a process of "creating" what is known.[121] This process involves both the individual being changed through his/her interaction with the environment and certain aspects of the environment being selected out and others ignored. One implication of this view is that a world of objects, which Dewey defines as "events with meaning,"[122] is not simply "sitting out there" waiting to be perceived, and that once perceived it is known. That particular point of view is what Dewey refers to as the "spectator theory of knowledge."[123] For Dewey our perceptual apparatus does not simply scan the face of our environment as a light shining over a darkened surface, seeing all it falls upon. Objects do not simply make their impressions on our waiting blank minds.[124] Against the spectator theory Dewey says that "things in their immediacy are unknown and unknowable, not because they are remote or behind some impenetrable veil of sensation of ideas, but because knowledge has no concern with them."[125] The term 'thing' thus refers to what has not yet been put into a context. If things are unknown it is because no one has bothered to know them yet, but in knowing them they will cease to be had in their immediacy. Things in their immediacy are unknowable simply because they have not acquired meaning through interaction with an individual. They are unrelated and exist in general. But we cannot know something in general, for that would require us to know it, but not as anything in particular. But knowing is specifically knowing things in particular, or organizing and relating things. Attaching meanings to things is what knowing is.[126]

However, each object does not simply have one way of being known, which it presents to us when we observe it.[127] The immediate object does not have some sort of real essence which it carries with it regardless of its station or use. This point is made clear by recalling that for Dewey the process of coming to know meaning is one and the same process with an individual's having his/her impulses mediated in certain specific ways rather than in others. This process as mentioned above, depends on the many accidental features of the situation.

From these comments it can be seen that the mind, or the what-it-is that is doing the knowing, is not a separate agency which simply takes in meanings, but an active element in the process of knowing.[128] For the same reason that impulses are never done being mediated, knowing something is not a single act which is done and finished; it is an ongoing process. The mind which knows is conditioned, and itself conditions. It conditions what is known through the process of selecting and adding meaning to the known. It is conditioned in the sense that knowing involves acquiring meanings through interaction with the environment. In explaining this relationship Dewey contrasts knowing, as a mental activity, with purely physical adjustment to the environment. Thus, he says:

> The difference between an adjustment to a physical stimulus and a *mental* act is that the latter involves response to a thing in its *meaning;* the former does not. A noise may make me jump without my mind being implicated. When I hear a noise and run and get water and put out a blaze, I respond intelligently....[129]

For Dewey the difference between the responses of the purely physical (inanimate) components of nature and those of psychophysical (animate) components is reflected in the consequences of those responses. Hence, he says "iron as such exhibits characteristics of bias or selective reactions, but it shows no bias in favor of remaining simple iron; it had just as soon, so to speak, become iron-oxide."[130] The components of nature which are thought of as having a "need" to maintain themselves, on the other hand, like living things, show an "activity of need-demand-satisfaction."[131] For Dewey the response difference between the animate and the inanimate with reference to consequences concerns modes of organization. Both can respond to outside stimulation, but the animate does so with the consequence that it tends to maintain itself.[132] Expressing the same point in another way, Dewey says, "My behavior has a mental quality. When things have a meaning for us, we *mean* (intend, propose) what we do: when they do not, we act blindly, unconsciously, unintelligently."[133]

In *Experience and Nature* Dewey sets out the meaning of the term 'mind' in a discussion of what he considers the traditional, though inauthentic, mind-body problem.[134] For the mind-body problem to be a problem in its traditional sense, a fundamental separation must be thought to exist between two separate realms of being: the mental or mind and the physical or body. Since the mind (according to the traditional view) is obviously not physical, for otherwise it would have the characteristics of other physical things (spatial location, observability) and yet we affirm that it exists, the problem is then to explain how the mind exists, in what way, and how it relates to the body. Traditional answers have taken many forms, from that of trying to reduce the mind to the body (materialism) or the body to the mind (idealism) to maintaining the separation between mind and body and trying to locate the process by which the interaction between the two unlike modes of being takes place.

The so-called mind-body problem is dealt with by Dewey by referring to the "body-mind" as a single event.[135] Thus it would be closer to the facts to say that Dewey *resolves* the mind-body problem rather than say that he *solved* it. Dewey resolves the problem by rejecting the problem as it has traditionally been conceived. It must be understood as a problem arising from the reification of terms used to relate processes like thinking or feeling into "things" such as thought or emotion. Once one has made the transition from talking of mental processes to talking of mind, it is already too late; the stage setting for the pseudo-problem (of how we are to conceive of the existence of this thing "mind") has already taken place. This is an example of what Dewey refers to as "*the* philosophical fallacy."[136]

For Dewey, the mind is not a psychical entity which interacts with a physical body. Rather he views mind in terms of behavior and says that mind

> represents something acquired. It represents reorganization of original activities through their operation in a given environment. It is a formation, not a datum; a product and a cause only after it has been produced.[137]

Further he states that

> what we call 'mind' means essentially the working of certain beliefs and desires; and that these in the concrete—in the only sense in which mind may be said to exist—are functions of associated behavior, varying with the structure and operation of social groups.[138]

In mentioning social groups, Dewey brings out a central point in his conception of mind. That mind is produced in an environment is Dewey's general position. However, when it is realized that the most important aspects of our environment consist in the other persons with whom we have contact, it becomes apparent that it is precisely our social environment which is most significant in the production of our mind. Accordingly, Dewey points out that

> *mind* as a concrete thing is precisely the power to understand things in terms of the use made of them; a socialized mind is the power to understand them in terms of the use to which they are turned in joint or shared situations.[139]

When the meanings which constitute mind become symbolized in language, they are no longer private or individual, but become 'social.' To that extent, for Dewey, mind also becomes social and comes under the control of the social environment. Thus Dewey says,

> the whole history of science, art and morals proves that the mind that appears *in* individuals is not as such individual mind. The former is in itself a system of belief, recognitions, and ignorances, acceptances and rejections, of expectancies and appraisals of meanings which have been instituted under the influence of custom and tradition.[140]

Dewey explains his point further by contrasting it with the traditional view. According to the latter view,

> thought [is] a purely inner activity, intrinsic to mind alone; and according to traditional classic doctrine, "mind" is complete and self-sufficient in itself. Overt action may follow upon its operations but in an external way, a way not intrinsic to its completion.[141]

The problem with the traditional view is that it leaves unexplained the question of social continuity mentioned at the outset of this chapter. Hence Dewey says:

> If we start with the traditional notion of mind as something complete in itself, then we may well be perplexed by the problem of how a common mind, common ways of feeling and believing and purposing, comes into existence.... [142]

In summary then, Dewey's view of the mind differs from many traditional views in that he returns mind to its place within nature rather than setting mind in opposition to nature. On this he says

> the mind is within the world as a part of the latter's own ongoing process. It is marked off as mind by the fact that wherever it is found, changes take place in a way, so that a movement in a definite one-way sense—from the doubtful and confused to the clear, resolved and settled— takes place.[143]

As previously mentioned, Dewey distinguishes the concept of mind or the mental from the concept of consciousness. If mind for Dewey consists essentially in the organized set of meanings which have been molded through our interactions with the environment, and which determines who we are, what then is the nature of consciousness?

In opening his discussion of consciousness in *Experience and Nature,* Dewey draws a distinction between two kinds of consciousness: consciousness *with meaning* and consciousness *without meaning.*[144] The term 'consciousness,' he says, is used in ordinary discourse to refer to either form of consciousness indifferently. The point here is apparently that one can be conscious without specific objects of knowledge within one's field of consciousness. This is not to say that we can be conscious without being conscious of anything, but only that the "anything" may simply be had as anything, unspecified for consciousness.[145] Consideration of the case of a newborn baby will lead one to understand how such consciousness without meanings can occur. Consciousness without meaning is the original consciousness which presents the occasion for meanings to be formed, and for consciousness with meaning to be evolved.[146]

If we ask for the status of the meanings which may or may not accompany consciousness, it becomes apparent that they must be part of our mental processes, or put metaphorically, they must exist "in our mind." This is what Dewey means when he says: "The greater part of mind is only implicit in any conscious act or state; the field of mind—of operative meanings—is enormously wider than that of consciousness. Mind is contextual and persistent; consciousness is focal and transitive."[147] The relationship of consciousness to mind makes clear why there must be two conceptions of consciousness, the one which conditions experience, the other which is itself conditioned. Consciousness with meaning is only possible because the mind is already there, supplying a framework "in back" of consciousness, to use another metaphor. The way a consciousness with meanings views experience, then, is totally dependent upon what particular meanings the mind holds in waiting, and these in turn depend upon the individual's past interactions with his/her environment.

The mind, however, could never obtain these meanings without consciousness. The idea of consciousness without meaning is thus something we can only conceive of and discuss long after it has ceased being *our* mode of consciousness. We can construct the state of "consciousness without meaning" logically, by reason, in the same way we can reason to the concepts of man's prehistoric past. Chronologically, consciousness without meaning (immediate consciousness) precedes consciousness with meaning, but, "it is impossible to tell what immediate consciousness is—not because there is some mystery in or behind it, but for the same reason that we cannot tell just what sweet or red immediately is: it is something had, not communicated and known."[148]

Dewey's understanding of what constitutes consciousness is related to, but distinguishable from, what he calls the "idealistic conception" of consciousness. On this view "consciousness [is thought of] as a power which modifies events...."[149] This conception, however, commits what Dewey calls the *philosophical fallacy* of taking the end result, that is, that which consciousness finally presents us with, events with meaning, and places that result into the mold of an antecedent condition.[150] Consciousness itself is not a power, but merely gives us the end result of a perception's interactions with the meanings supplied by the mind.

In addition to relating his own view to that of the idealistic tradition, Dewey refers his view to the "realist doctrine" for contrast as well. The realist doctrine holds that "consciousness is like the eye running over a field of ready-made objects...."[151] The problem with this view is that it conceives of events as prelabeled with respect to their own inherent significance. But for Dewey "the fact that something is an occurrence does not decide what kind of an occurrence it is.... To argue from an experience 'being an experience' to what it is of and about is warranted by no logic."[152]

As frequently becomes apparent when Dewey examines philosophical problems in their historical context, each side has grasped part of the whole and tried to make it do for the whole itself. Put the two views (idealism and realism) together and the resulting view does not have the simplicity of either, but it does have the conceptual power to clarify the complex notion of "being conscious of." When we become conscious of a particular object, this is only possible because we were first aware of a certain event which took on a certain meaning and thus qualified itself as knowable. Things do not come "ready-made" with all their significance into our conscious field, nor is our consciousness responsible for the original production of what we are aware of.

One significant aspect of Dewey's view of consciousness can be found in the implications it has for dealing with the traditional empiricist epistemological conception which distinguishes inner from outer modes of consciousness. According to Dewey, the usual practice in talking of consciousness is to distinguish consciousness taken as the perception of "real things now existing in the world,"[153] from other types of consciousness. The mistake in this view, according to Dewey, appears as the prejudice in favor of sense perception as a more veridical mode of consciousness. Placing this prejudice in the context of what has already been said of consciousness it appears without foundation. This is the case because perception of objects involves the events which are taking place in the world plus the fund of meanings with which the mind has been stocked. Other modes of consciousness like "emotion, thinking, remembering, fancy and imagination"[154] have the same status in consciousness as each other and perception, because each "in its immediate existence is exactly the same sort of thing, namely a remaking of meanings of events."[155]

This is perhaps a part of what Kant intended when he made his famous assertion that "existence is not a real predicate."[156] The consciousness of something is not altered as consciousness of something by additional knowledge that what one is conscious of exists. This is not to deny that how a state of consciousness functions may alter what a person does, but the consciousness *qua* consciousness will be the same before we attempt to verify whether what we are conscious of exists or not. If this were not the case, such verifications would be as useless as they are unnecessary; they would be useless for the verification would reveal no new knowledge; they would be unnecessary because if we could find a clue within the consciousness itself as to whether the intentional object of consciousness existed, no verification would be required. Thus Dewey says: "To discover that a perception or an idea is cognitively invalid is to find that the consequences which follow from acting upon it entangle and confuse the other consequences which follow from the causes of the perception, instead of integrating or coordinating harmoniously with them."[157] To clarify this point Dewey says, "the difference, it is implied, between awareness of present and 'real' things and of absent and unreal is extrinsic, not intrinsic to a consciousness."[158]

A result of the fact that different modes of consciousness have the same epistemological status as one another (as modes of consciousness) is that for Dewey

> the same existential events are capable of an infinite number of meanings. The existence identified as "paper," because the meaning uppermost at the moment is "something to be written upon," has as many other explicit meanings as it has important consequences recognized in the various connective interactions into which it enters.[159]

Further Dewey says:

> Immediately, every perceptual awareness may be termed
> indifferently emotion, sensation, thought, desire: not
> that it *is* immediately any one of these, or all of them
> combined, but that when it is taken in some *reference,*
> to conditions or to consequences or to *both,* it has in that
> contextual reference, the distinctive properties of emo-
> tion, sensation, thought or desire.[160]

Concerning Dewey's views on consciousness, then, it should be
noticed that consciousness is not an entity for Dewey. On the contrary, as
Dewey points out, consciousness is not "an underlying substance, cause,
or source. It [is rather] a specifiable quality of some forms of behavior."[161]
This specifiable quality is found in the ability of individuals to respond to
aspects of their environments in what can be described as intelligent ways.
Intelligent response consists, for Dewey, in responding to events and
objects in terms of their meanings, rather than as bare occurrences. Thus
Dewey says

> [the] use of one change or perceptible occurrence as a
> sign of others and as a means of preparing ourselves,
> did not wait for the development of modern science. It
> is as old as man himself, being the heart of all intelli-
> gence.[162]

And further:

> Intelligence... is associated with judgment; that is, with
> selection and arrangement of means to effect conse-
> quences and with choice of what we take as our ends. A
> man is intelligent not in virtue of having reason which
> grasps first and indemonstrable truths about fixed prin-
> ciples, in order to reason deductively from them to the
> particulars which they govern, but in virtue of his
> capacity to estimate the possibilities of a situation and
> to act in accordance with his estimate....Wherever
> intelligence operates, things are judged in their capacity
> of signs of other things.[163]

Intelligence, for Dewey, is a concept which relates the different
aspects of his psychological analysis: impulse, habit, mind, and consciousness. Hence, for Dewey:

> What intelligence has to do in the service of impulse is
> to act not as its obedient servant but as its clarifier and
> liberator. And this can be accomplished only by a study
> of the conditions and causes, the workings and conse-
> quences of the greatest possible variety of desires and
> combinations of desires. Intelligence converts desire
> into plans, systematic plans based on assembling facts,
> reporting events as they happen, keeping tab on them
> and analyzing them.[164]

It should be noted that for Dewey, intelligence is understood in a behavioristic way. It is not a force or entity but a way of behaving. On this score Dewey says "intelligence is not an outside power presiding supremely but statically over the desires and efforts of man, but is a method of adjustment of capacities and conditions within specific situations."[165]

In its most general terms, intelligence is a form of behavior which is organized and directed toward the solution of problems. It is not, as understood in some traditional psychologies, an innate capacity which underlies and causes certain forms of behavior. The intelligence of behavior is found only in the form which actual activities take. Intelligent behavior is that which is able to adjust and grow with changes in the environment. Dewey says of intelligence in this most general sense that

> it is a shorthand designation for great and ever growing
> methods of observation, experiment and reflective rea-
> soning which have in a very short time revolutionized
> the physical and, to a considerable degree, the physi-
> ological conditions of life, but which have not as yet
> been worked out for application to what is itself distinc-
> tively and basically human.[166]

Dewey's reference in this last statement is in part to the lack of intelligence which has been practiced in ethical or moral matters, and this, in part, is the topic of Chapter Three.

8. Deliberation, Choice, and Will

Much of the concern of ethics is with presenting and analyzing the justifications for moral decisions. Since this is the case, it is imperative that the nature of the deliberative process be made explicit. The need for deliberation in a given situation is not idle, for Dewey, but is called forth by some conflict in desires, impulses, or values. This implies that before there can be deliberation there already must be some basis of valuation— some values which have gone unquestioned until they came into conflict. Put another way, deliberation cannot be about everything in general, it must begin with certain aspects of a situation which are accepted.[167] On this Dewey points out that:

> Prior to anything which may be called choice in the sense of deliberate decision come spontaneous selections or *preferences*. Every appetite and impulse, however blind, is a mode of preferring one thing to another; it selects one thing and rejects others. It goes out with attraction to certain objects, putting them ahead of others in value. The latter are neglected although from a purely external standpoint they are equally accessible and available. We are so constructed that both by original temperament and by acquired habit we move toward some objects rather than others. Such preference antecedes judgment of comparative value; it is organic rather than conscious. Afterwards there arise situations in which wants compete; we are drawn spontaneously in opposite directions.[168]

And further that:

> It is a great error to suppose that we have no preferences until there is a choice. We are always biased beings, tending in one direction rather than another. The occasion of deliberation is an *excess* of preferences, not natural apathy or an absence of likings. We want things that are incompatible with one another; therefore we have to make a choice of what we really want, of the course of action, that is, which most fully releases activities.[169]

When such a situation arises, deliberation ideally involves the sorting out of alternatives and the determination of the means to each alternative, plus its probable consequences.[170] One of the significant points in favor of carrying through a process of deliberation prior to making a choice is that one gets some indication of how he/she will feel about the choice once it is actually made. This is so for Dewey since "any actual experience of reflection upon conduct will show that every foreseen result at once stirs our present affections, our likes and dislikes, our desires and aversions."[171]

Put another way, what occurs during deliberation, according to Dewey, is an imaginative presentation of possibilities with their consequences and conditions of production, and an experiencing of feelings corresponding to each possible choice. Thus for Dewey,

> deliberation is a process of active, suppressed, rehearsal; of imaginative dramatic performance of various deeds carrying to their appropriate issues the various tendencies which we feel stirring within us. When we see in imagination this or that change brought about, there is a direct sense of the amount and kind of worth which attaches to it, as real and as direct, if not as strong, as if the act were really performed and its consequences really brought home to us.[172]

There are at least three significant outcomes of this conception of deliberation, according to Dewey. One of these is that deliberation makes intelligent choice possible. Because we imaginatively rehearse the possibilities before us, we lessen the need for performing acts for which we will later feel regret. "The advantage of a mental trial, prior to the overt trial (for the act after all is itself also a trial, a proving of the idea that lies back of it)," according to Dewey, "is that it is retrievable, whereas overt consequences remain. They cannot be recalled."[173]

A second outcome of Dewey's analysis of deliberation that it corrects the mistaken, but widely accepted, conception of deliberation presented by the utilitarians in the nineteenth century. The utilitarian picture of deliberation was concerned with the imaginative weighing of future pleasures and displeasures in an attempt to reach the best solution to a moral problem. But according to Dewey,

> when we analyze what occurs, we find that this process of comparing future possible satisfactions, to see which is the greater, takes place on exactly the opposite basis from that set forth by Bentham. We do not compare results in the way of fixed amounts of pleasures and pains, but we compare *objective* results, changes to be effected in ourselves, *in* others, in the whole social situation; during this comparison desires and aversions

take more definite form and strength, so that we find the idea of one result more agreeable, more harmonious, to our present character than another. *Then* we say it is more satisfying, it affords more pleasure than another.[174]

The third point concerns the potential significance of any deliberation, when it is seen as a means of altering the character of self. The deliberation leading to a particular choice is not merely deliberation as to specific actions, it is also, at least in germ, deliberation as to the kind of person one chooses to be. On this Dewey says:

Now every such choice [between competing desires] sustains a double relation to the self. It reveals the existing self and it forms the future self. That which is chosen is that which is found congenial to the desires and habits of the self as it already exists. Deliberation has an important function in this process, because each different possibility as it is presented to the imagination appeals to a different element in the constitution of the self, thus giving all sides of character a chance to play their part in the final choice. The resulting choice also shapes the self, making it, in some degree, a new self. This fact is especially marked at critical junctures, but it marks every choice to some extent however slight.[175]

Since deliberation is called forth initially by some blockage to action because of a conflict of values, its close must release the individual to a particular course of action. This ending of deliberation is referred to as choice. The path is cleared for choice through deliberation, as described above. A choice is reached when, through the process of deliberation, one course of action is seen to be more consistent with the self or character than the alternatives. This may only happen when both the conditions and consequences of each possible choice are imagined, both in relation to the present and possible self. According to Dewey, choice involves

simply hitting in imagination upon an object which furnishes an adequate stimulus to the recovery of overt action. Choice is made as soon as some habit, or some combination of elements of habits and impulse, finds a way fully open.[176]

The will, for Dewey, is not a separate part of the self, but is another name for the effective integration of the self which takes place when one is able to carry through a process of deliberation to arrive at a choice and then put the choice into action. The "will" according to Dewey, "signifies an active tendency to foresee consequences, to form resolute purposes, and to use all the efforts at command to produce the intended consequences in fact."[177] Thus it can be seen that the importance of will, for Dewey, is that it is an index of personal effectiveness and integration of character.

Given Dewey's view of will, it can be seen why he was not concerned with the doctrine of "freedom of the will." The freedom necessary to make intelligent decisions is not a metaphysical freedom of the will, but a matter of knowledge.[178] "Insistence upon a metaphysical freedom of will is generally at its most strident pitch," according to Dewey, "with those who despise knowledge of matters-of-fact."[179] As a measure of the kind of freedom which is desirable in deliberation, Dewey suggests that we look to our ability to see the alternative courses of action and evaluate them in an intelligent and unprejudiced manner.

> What we want [according to Dewey] is possibilities open in the *world* not in the will, except as will or deliberate activity reflects the world. To foresee future objective alternatives and to be able by deliberation to choose one of them and thereby weigh its chances in the struggle for future existence, measures our freedom.[180]

9. Education, Growth, and Development

The overall psychological process through which an individual progresses through his/her life can be seen, according to Dewey, as a process of education, growth, and development. These three concepts are closely related. Education happens when an individual interacts with his/her environment and as a result is able to interact with the environment more effectively in the future. The result of such education is the growth and development of the individual. According to Dewey, "life is development, and...developing, growing is life. Translated into its educational equivalents, this means (i) that the educational process has no end beyond itself; it is its own end; and that (ii) the educational process is one of continual reorganizing, reconstructing, transforming."[181] Put differently, "growth," according to Dewey, is not a capacity to take on change of form in accord with external pressure.... It is essentially the ability to learn from experience; the power to retain from one experience something which is of avail in coping with the difficulties of a later situation. This means power to modify actions on the basis of the results of prior experiences, the power to *develop dispositions*. Without it, the acquisition of habits *is* impossible.[182]

When Dewey contends that education is the basis of growth, and that growth is an end, he is not using the term 'education' in its popular sense of "acquiring information."[183] The education with which Dewey is concerned is the actual transformation of character, not a mere storing of facts.

Education for Dewey involves the mediation of impulses and the formation and decomposition of habits. It is not something to be equated with what goes on in school but rather with a lifelong activity, beginning when life itself begins. Education takes place through an individual's interaction with his/her environment, and it involves a transformation wherein more and more aspects of the environment take on meaning. When education is institutionalized the same principle holds true. Thus Dewey says:

> We never educate directly, but indirectly by means of the environment. Whether we permit chance environments to do the work, or whether we design environments for the purpose makes a great difference. And any environment is a chance environment so far as its educative influence is concerned unless it has been deliberately regulated with reference to its educative effect.[184]

Although education and growth are psychological concerns, for Dewey they are just as much moral concerns. The fact that in his psychology Dewey sees growth as an end in no way precludes his stressing the moral significance of growth and hence education. The moral significance of Dewey's psychological theory will be taken up in the next chapter.

Endnotes

[1] John Dewey, "The Need for Social Psychology," *Psychological Review* 24 (July 1917): 275. Dewey notes the redundancy of referring to "social" psychology in this same article, p. 268.

[2] John Dewey, *Psychology* (New York: Harper and Brothers, 1989); reprinted in *The Early Works of John Dewey, 1882-1.8.98*, George E. Axtelle, et al., eds., 5 vols. (Carbondale and Edwardsville: Southern Illinois University Press, 1969), 2:11.

[3] Ibid., pp. 13-16.

[4] John Dewey, "The New Psychology," *Andover Review* 2 (Sept. 1884); reprinted in *The Early Works of John Dewey, 1882-1898*, George E. Axtelle, et al., eds., 5 vols. (Carbondale and Edwardsville: Southern Illinois University Press, 1969), 1:55.

[5] Ibid., p. 48.

[6] Dewey, *Psychology*, pp. 14-15.

[7] Dewey, "The New Psychology," p. 57.

[8] Ibid., p. 48.

[9] John Dewey, "The Psychological Standpoint," *Mind* 11 (Jan. 1886); reprinted in *The Early Works of John Dewey, 1882-1898*, George E. Axtelle, et al., eds., 5 vols. (Carbondale and Edwardsville: Southern Illinois University Press, 1969), 1:123.

[10] John Dewey, "Psychology as Philosophic Method," *Mind* 11 (April 1886); reprinted in *The Early Works of John Dewey 1882-898*, George E. Axtelle, et al., eds., 5 vols. (Carbondale and Edwardsville: Southern Illinois University Press, 1969), 1:149.

[11] Ibid., p. 156.

[12] On this Dewey says, "But the whole history of science, art and morals proves that the mind that appears *in* individuals is not as such individual mind" *(Experience and Nature*, p. 219). Further, he says:

> In his [Hegel's] philosophy of history and society culminated the efforts of a whole series of German writers—Lessing, Herder, Kant, Schiller, Goethe—to appreciate the nurturing influence of the great collective institutional products of humanity. For those who learned the lesson of this movement, it was henceforth impossible to conceive of institutions or of culture as artificial. It destroyed completely—in idea, not in fact—the psychology that regarded "mind" as a ready-made possession of a naked individual by showing the significance of "objective mind"—language, government, art, religion—in the formation of individual minds *(Democracy and Education* [New York: The Macmillan Company, 1916] ,p. 69).

[13] John Dewey, "From Absolutism to Experimentalism," in *Contemporary American Philosophers*, George Plimpton Adams and William Pepperell Montague, eds. (New York: Macmillan Company, 1930), p. 23.

[14] See, for example, Neil Coughlan, *Young John Dewey* (Chicago: The University of Chicago Press, 1975), chapters 4, 8, and 9; and George Dykhuizen, *The Life and Mind of John Dewey* (Carbondale and Edwardsville: Southern Illinois University Press, 1973), pp. 68-71.

[15] Dewey, "From Absolutism to Experimentalism," p. 23.

[16] Ibid., p. 11.

[17] John Dewey, *Philosophy and Civilization* (New York: Minton, Balch and Company, 1931), p. 27; first published, "Le Développement du Pragmatisme Américain," *Revue de*

métaphysique et de morale 19: 411-430; retranslated into English and published as "The Development of American Pragmatism," *Studies in the History of Ideas* 2:. 353-357.

[18] Dewey, *Psychology*, p. 11.

[19] Dewey, "The Need for Social Psychology," p. 270. Dewey explains his hesitancy to use the term 'introspection' and his preference for 'inspection' because "'introspection' is too heavily charged with meanings derived from the animistic tradition." ("Conduct and Experience," in *Psychologies of 1930*, edited by Carl Murchison [Worcester, *Mass.: Clark* University Press, 1930], p. 416).

[20] Dewey, "The Need for Social Psychology," p. 272.

[21] Ibid., p. 276.

[22] Ibid., p. 269.

[23] Ibid., p. 268.

[24] Ibid., p. 246.

[25] Dewey, *Human Nature and Conduct*, p. 85.

[26] Ibid.

[27] Dewey, "The Need for Social Psychology," p. 275.

[28] Ibid., p. 271.

[29] Ibid., p. 270.

[30] Coughlan, *Young John Dewey*, pp. 136-137.

[31] John Dewey, "The Reflex Arc Concept in Psychology," *Psychological Review* 3 (July 1896); reprinted in *The Early Works of John Dewey, 1882-1898*, George E. Axtelle, et al., 5 vols. (Carbondale and Edwardsville: Southern Illinois University Press, 1972), 5:96.

[32] Ibid., p. 105. For a discussion of this fallacy see Dewey, *Experience and Nature*, p. 68.

[33] Dewey, "The Reflex Arc Concept in Psychology," p. 100.

[34] Ibid., p. 99.

[35] Ibid., p. 98.

[36] John Dewey, *The Study of Ethics: A Syllabus*, (Ann Arbor, Michigan: Register Publishing Company, 1894); reprinted in *The Early Works of John Dewey, 1882-1898*, George E. Axtelle, et al., eds., 5 vols. (Carbondale and Edwardsville: Southern Illinois University Press, 1971), 4:237. In the same work he says "the mediation of the impulse thus means a process of self development. It is the process by which the self becomes aware of the meaning, in terms of its own experiences, of one of its own impulses" (p. 243).

[37] Ibid., p 237

[38] Dewey, "The Reflex Arc Concept in Psychology," p. 98.

[39] Ibid., p. 96.

[40] Ibid., p. 102.

[41] Ibid., p. 101.

[42] Ibid.

[43] Ibid.

[44] Dewey, *Logic*, p. 25. cf. *The Study of Ethics: A Syllabus*, pp. 232-233; *Outlines of a Critical Theory of Ethics* (Ann Arbor, Michigan: Register Publishing Company, 1891), pp. 99-100;

see also, "Conduct and Experience," p. 411.

[45] Dewey, *Democracy and Education*, p. 13.

[46] Dewey, *Logic*, p. 25.

[47] Dewey, *Democracy and Education*, p. 13.

[48] Ibid., p. 26.

[49] Dewey, *The Quest for Certainty*, p. 224.

[50] Dewey, *Logic*, p. 25.

[51] Ibid., p. 26.

[52] Ibid., p. 27.

[53] Ibid.

[54] Ibid.

[55] Ibid.

[56] Ibid.

[57] Dewey, *Democracy and Education*, p. 30.

[58] Dewey, *Logic*, p. 29.

[59] Ibid.

[60] Ibid.

[61] Ibid., p. 29-30.

[62] John Dewey, *Art as Experience* (New York:Minton, Baich and Company, 1934), p. 58.

[63] Ibid., p. 58.

[64] Ibid., p. 60.

[65] Dewey, *Human Nature and Conduct*, p. 105.

[66] Ibid., pp. 110-112.

[67] John Dewey, *The Public and its Problems* (New York: Henry, Holt and Company, 1927), p. 10.

[68] Dewey, *The Study of Ethics: A Syllabus*, p. 235.

[69] To clarify this point Dewey says "the original or natural impulse is completely *transformed;* it no longer exists in its first condition; our impulse to locomotion for example is entirely made over when the reaction of other experiences into it is completed—when we learn to walk...." (Ibid., p. 240).

[70] Ibid., p. 243.

[71] Ibid., p. 235.

[72] Dewey, *Human Nature and Conduct*, pp. 254-255.

[73] Ibid., p. 95.

[74] Dewey, *The Study of Ethics:A Syllabus*, p. 236.

[75] Ibid.

[76] Ibid.

[77] On this point Dewey states,

> Disposition is habitual, persistent. It shows itself therefore in many acts and in many consequences. Only as we keep a running account, can we judge disposition,

disentangling its tendency from accidental accompaniments. When once we have got a fair idea of its tendency, we are able to place the particular consequences of a single act in a wider context of continuing consequences (*Human Nature and Conduct*, pp. 45-46).

[78] Dewey, *The Study of Ethics: A Syllabus*, p. 241.

[79] Ibid., p. 238.

[80] Dewey, *Outlines of a Critical Theory of Ethics*, p. 22. On this Dewey also says "every conscious act, in its lowest terms, is a mediated impulse—'mediation' being the reference back to an impulse of the experiences which it is likely to occasion" *(The Study of Ethics: A Syllabus*, p. 240). And also, "impulse goes straight and blindly at an end, but it does not know this end, nor does it feel that there will be pleasure in reaching it" *(Psychology*, p. 310).

[81] Dewey, *Psychology*, p. 312.

[82] Dewey, *Outlines of a Critical Theory of* Ethics, pp. 18-19.

[83] Dewey further states,

desire is the forward urge of living creatures. When the push and drive of life meets no obstacle, there is just life-activity. But obstructions present themselves, and activity is dispersed and divided. Desire is the outcome. It is the activity surging forward to break through what dams it up. The "object" which then presents itself in thought as the goal of desire is the object of the environment *which, if it were present*, would secure a reunification of activity and the restoration of its ongoing activity *(Human Nature and Conduct*, pp. 249-250).

[84] Ibid., p. 250. See also, John Dewey, *Theory of Valuation* ("International Encyclopedia of Unified Science," Otto Neurath, et al., eds., vol. 2, no. 4; Chicago: The University of Chicago Press, 1933), p. 33; and *The Quest for Certainty*, p. 35.

[85] Dewey, *Democracy and Education*, pp. 54-55. See also, Dewey and Tufts, *Ethics* (New York: Henry Holt and Company, 1908), pp. 342-343.

[86] Dewey, *The Study of Ethics: A Syllabus*, p. 241.

[87] Dewey, *Human Nature and Conduct*, p. 172. In the same discussion Dewey says "without habit there is only irritation and confused hesitation. With habit alone there is a machine-like repetition, a duplicating recurrence of old acts. With conflict of habits and release of impulse there is conscious search" (p. 180).

[88] Dewey states, "The more numerous our habits, the wider is the field of possible observation and foretelling. The more flexible they are, the more refined is perception in its discrimination and the more delicate the presentation evoked in imagination" (Ibid., pp. 175-176).

[89] Ibid., p. 42.

[90] Dewey, *Democracy and Education*, p. 35.

[91] Ibid., p. 57. See also, Dewey, *Human Nature and Conduct*, p. 177.

[92] Dewey and Tufts, *Ethics* (1932), p. 181.

[93] Dewey, *Human Nature and Conduct*, p. 24.

[94] Ibid., pp. 40-41.

[95] Dewey, *The Problems of Men*, p. 229.

[96] Dewey, *The Study of Ethics: A Syllabus*, p. 242.

[97] Dewey and Tufts, *Ethics* (1932), pp. 178-179.

[98] Ibid., p. 181.

[99] Ibid., pp. 181-182.

[100] Dewey defines character as follows: "Character is that body of active tendencies and interests in the individual which make him open, ready, warm to certain aims, and callous, cold, blind to others, and which accordingly habitually tend to make him acutely aware of and favorable to certain sorts of consequences, and ignorant of or hostile to other consequences" (Dewey and Tufts, *Ethics*, p. 255).

[101] Dewey and Tufts, *Ethics* (1932), p. 183. cf. Dewey and Tufts, *Ethics* (1908), pp. 261-261; Dewey, *Outlines of a Critical Theory of Ethics*, pp. 9-10; Dewey, *The Study of Ethics: A Syllabus*, p. 241; Dewey, "Conduct and Experience," p. 412; Dewey and Tufts, *Ethics* (1932), p. 184.

[102] Dewey and Tufts, *Ethics* (1932), p. 340.

[103] Dewey, *Human Nature and Conduct*, p. 138.

[104] Ibid., p. 119.

[105] Ibid.

[106] Dewey, *Psychology*, p. 315.

[107] Dewey and Tufts, *Ethics* (1932), p. 320.

[108] Ibid., p. 321.

[109] Ibid., p. 186.

[110] Dewey, *The Study of Ethics: A Syllabus*, pp. 242-243.

[111] Dewey, *Human Nature and Conduct*, p. 120.

[112] Dewey and Tufts, *Ethics* (1932), p. 322.

[113] Dewey, *Human Nature and Conduct*, p. 120.

[114] Dewey and Tufts, *Ethics* (1932), p. 185.

[115] Dewey, *Experience and Nature*, p. 267.

[116] Dewey and Tufts, *Ethics* (1932), p. 185.

[117] Ibid.

[118] Dewey, *Human Nature and Conduct*, p. 76.

[119] Dewey and Tufts, *Ethics* (1932), p. 186.

[120] See, for example, Dewey, *Democracy and Education*, p. 36.

[121] Dewey, *The Quest for Certainty*, p. 204. Dewey says "knowing is seen to be a participant in what is finally known."

[122] Dewey, *Experience and Nature*, p. 318.

[123] Dewey, *The Quest for Certainty*, p. 23.

[124] Dewey takes a behavioristic view of knowledge. He says, for example, "knowledge which is not projected against the black unknown lives in the muscles, not in consciousness" (*Human Nature and Conduct*, p. 177). See also, Dewey, *The Quest for Certainty*, pp. 167-168, *227-229*, and 291.

[125] Dewey, *Experience and Nature*, p. 86.

[126] See, for example, Dewey, *Experience and Nature*, p. 128.

[127] Ibid., p. 236. In the same discussion Dewey says "different manners of experiencing affect the status of the subject-matter experienced."

128 Ibid., p. 14. Cf. Dewey, *The Quest for Certainty,* pp. 165-167 and p. 204; Dewey, "Experience, Knowledge and Value," p. 564.

129 Dewey, *Democracy and Education,* p. 35.

130 Dewey, *Experience and Nature,* p. 254.

131 Ibid.

132 Ibid., pp. 253-254.

133 Dewey, *Democracy and Education,* p. 35.

134 Dewey, *Experience and Nature,* Chapters 6 and 7.

135 Ibid., p. 255.

136 Ibid., pp. 8 and 29.

137 Dewey, "The Need for Social Psychology," pp 271-272. See also, Dewey, *Democracy and Education,* p. 39.

138 Dewey, "The Need for Social Psychology," p. 272.

139 Dewey, *Democracy and Education,* pp. 39-40.

140 Dewey, *Experience and Nature,* p. 219.

141 Dewey, *The Quest for Certainty,* pp. 7-8. Dewey also notes that

the most popular forms of... psycho-analysis, retain the notion of a separate psychic realm or force. They add a statement pointing to facts of the utmost value, and which is equivalent to practical recognition of the dependence of mind upon habit and of habit upon social conditions. This is the statement of the existence and operation of the 'unconscious,' of complexes due to contacts and conflicts with others, of the social, censor. But they still cling to the idea of the separate psychic realm and so in effect talk about unconscious consciousness. They get their truths mixed up in theory with the false psychology of original individual consciousness.... (*Human Nature and Conduct,* pp. 86-87).

142 Dewey, *Human Nature and Conduct,* p. 61.

143 Dewey, *The Quest for Certainty,* p. 291.

144 Dewey, *Experience and Nature,* p. 298.

145 Ibid., pp. 3-4.

146 Ibid., p. 343.

147 Ibid., p. 303.

148 Ibid., p. 307.

149 Ibid., p. 308.

150 Ibid.

151 Ibid.

152 Ibid., p. 1.

153 Ibid., p. 318.

154 Ibid.

155 Ibid.

156 Immanuel Kant, *Critique of Pure Reason,* translated by Norman Kemp Smith (London: Macmillan and Company, 1929), p. 504.

[157] Dewey, *Experience and Nature*, pp. 323-324.

[158] Ibid., p. 318.

[159] Ibid., p. 319.

[160] Ibid., pp. 304-305.

[161] Dewey,"Conduct and Experience," p. 416.

[162] Dewey, *The Quest for Certainty*, p. 132.

[163] Ibid., p. 213.

[164] Dewey, *Human Nature and Conduct*, p. 255.

[165] Dewey, *The Influence of Darwin on Philosophy*, p. 68. See also, Dewey and Tufts, *Ethics* (1908), p. 306.

[166] Dewey, *Reconstruction in Philosophy* (1948 introduction), pp. viii-ix.

[167] See, for example, Dewey, *Logic*, p. 108.

[168] Dewey and Tufts, *Ethics* (1932), p. 316.

[169] Dewey, *Human Nature and Conduct*, p. 193.

[170] See Dewey, *Theory of Valuation*, p. 25.

[171] Dewey and Tufts, *Ethics* (1908), p. 323; Dewey and Tufts, *Ethics* (1932), p. 303.

[172] Dewey and Tufts, *Ethics* (1908), pp. 322-323. See also p. 323; Dewey and Tufts, *Ethics* (1932), p. 303.

[173] Dewey and Tufts, *Ethics* (1908), pp. 323-324; Dewey and Tufts, *Ethics* (1932), p. 303.

[174] Dewey and Tufts, *Ethics* (1908), p. 277.

[175] Dewey and Tufts, *Ethics* (1932), p. 317.

[176] Dewey, *Human Nature and Conduct*, p. 192.

[177] Dewey and Tufts, *Ethics* (1932), p. 187.

[178] Dewey, *Human Nature and Conduct*, p. 311.

[179] Ibid., p. 305.

[180] Ibid., p. 311.

[181] Dewey, *Democracy and Education*, p. 59.

[182] Ibid., pp. 52-53.

[183] Ibid., p. 60.

[184] Ibid., p. 22.

CHAPTER THREE

DEWEY'S ETHICS

The last chapter dealt with Dewey's psychological views and stressed Dewey's rejection of mentalistic explanations as well as his emphasis on outward behavioral aspects of human psychology. However, Dewey's psychology was not presented for its own sake, but rather for the purpose giving a fuller understanding of his ethical beliefs. The present chapter deals with those ethical beliefs and shows how they grow out of his psychological theory.

As noted in the first chapter, Dewey held to the belief that ethical theory, to be of any practical value, must base itself upon the best available psychological data. This is not to say, however, that Dewey believed that ethics can be reduced to psychology, or that it is merely a branch of that science. Thus Dewey says, for example:

> Psychological analysis does not...set before us an end or ideal actually experienced, whether moral or otherwise. It does not purport to tell us *what* the end or ideal is. But psychological analysis shows us just what forming and entertaining an end means. Psychological analysis abstracts from the concrete make-up of an end, as that is found as a matter of direct experience, and because of (not in spite of) that abstraction sets before us having-an-end in terms of its conditions and its effects, that is, in terms of taking other characteristic attitudes which *are present in* other experiences.[1]

Though ethics cannot be reduced to psychology, Dewey was firm on his statement that the information psychology can supply is essential to effective ethical theory. Hence, Dewey points out that

> purely psychologic propositions are indispensable to any concrete moral theory. The logical analysis of the process of moral judgment, setting forth its inherent organization or structure with reference to the peculiar logical function it has to accomplish, furnishes the categories or limiting terms of ethical science, and supplies their formal meaning, their definition.[2]

The significance of recognizing the proper relationship between psychological and ethical theory is, for Dewey, however, dependent upon the nature or quality of the psychological theory in question. The psychological theory used to support ethical theory must represent the most adequate account of human behavior available. However, as Dewey points out in the *Theory of Valuation:*

> Psychological science is now in much the same state in which astronomy, physics, and chemistry were when they first emerged as genuinely experimental sciences, yet without such a science systematic theoretical control of valuation is impossible; for without competent psychological knowledge the force of the human factors which interact with environing nonhuman conditions to produce consequences cannot be estimated.[3]

Thus, though Dewey wanted to base his ethical theory on sound psychological footing, he was also aware that psychology itself was only beginning to emerge from its speculative and introspective past. As previously noted, the truly experimental psychology which he saw as offering the kind of information required in ethical theory was a behavioristic psychology, but such a psychology was far from achieving general acceptance; the older introspective psychology was still much in evidence. Thus the situation in ethical theory contained the ironic circumstance that even were an ethical theorist to take seriously Dewey's advise to base ethical theory upon psychological data, the widely accepted psychological perspective was still introspective and mentalistic in outlook. In *Human Nature and Conduct* Dewey notes this irony:

> Any moral theory which is seriously influenced by
> current psychological theory is bound to emphasize
> states of consciousness, an inner private life, at the
> expense of acts which have public meaning and which
> incorporate and exact social relationships.[4]

As stressed in the last chapter, Dewey went far in freeing himself from
the older mentalistic psychology, and thus the irony just mentioned did not
seriously affect his own thinking. It is interesting to note, however, that
Dewey's critics often failed to realize the latter point, and as a result
accused him of inconsistencies which only would have been such had he
not rejected the mentalistic form of psychological explanation.[5] As a result
of his acceptance of a behavioristic rather than a mentalistic psychology,
he was able to follow his own advice and base his ethical theory upon, or
rather within, what he took to be a sound psychological context.

1. The Moral Situation and Moral Theory

Moral theory begins, for Dewey, where all forms of inquiry begin:
with a problem or problematic situation.[6] According to Dewey, *"moral
conceptions and processes grow naturally out of the very conditions of
human life."*[7] Further he says "the fundamental conceptions of morals are
neither arbitrary nor artificial. They are not imposed upon human nature
from without but develop out of its own operations and needs."[8] Above all,
for Dewey, ethical theory is not merely "theoretical." "If inquiries are to
have any substantial basis," according to Dewey, "the theorist must take
his departure from the problems which men actually meet in their own
conduct."[9]

The kinds of problems which moral theory is concerned with, though
referred to as moral problems, are not a rare form of problem set apart from
those of day-to-day life. The belief that moral problems are unusual and
uncommon would, if true, make moral or ethical theory pointless from
Dewey's perspective. What gives moral theory its urgency is the fact that
everyone's life is filled with moral problems. Dewey emphasizes this
point when he says, "the first step in ethics is to fix firmly in mind the idea
that the term moral does not mean any special or peculiar kind of conduct,
but simply means practice and action, conduct viewed not partially, but in
connection with the end which it realizes."[10] In general, "morals," according to Dewey, "has to do with all activity into which alternative possibilities enter. For wherever they enter, a difference between better and worse
arises."[11]

When it is recognized that Dewey's use of the term 'moral' is broad enough to take in all situations where considerations of better and worse arise, it is not surprising that for him all conduct is potentially moral.[12] That this is the case may be seen from two related perspectives.

First, as defined in the last chapter, conduct is human behavior viewed in its interrelatedness. Conduct, that is, is not made up of isolated actions, but rather of actions leading from and leading to other actions. The actions we perform today help to explicate the meanings of actions we performed yesterday. Tomorrow's actions will help demonstrate the meanings implicit in today's actions. Concerning this point Dewey says:

> "Present" activity is not a sharp narrow knife blade in time. The present is complex, containing within itself a multitude of habits and impulses. It is enduring, a course of action, a process including memory, observation and foresight, a pressure forward, a glance backward and a look outward. It is of *moral* moment because it marks a transition in the direction of breadth and clarity of action or in that of triviality and confusion.[13]

Because of this, all actions have potential moral value, since they may set us on courses of conduct leading to moral decisions. The actions which are instrumental in producing explicit moral choices can no more be stripped of their moral significance than any element in a cause-and-effect chain can be abstracted and claimed to be uninvolved in the outcome. The second reason why all our conduct has potential moral significance has to do with character and character formation. In the discussion of Dewey's psychology it was mentioned that a person's character is the sum of his/her habitual modes of behavior. A person's habits are the result of fulfilling certain impulses in certain regular ways. In fulfilling impulses one's character is given shape. Therefore, according to Dewey, "every act is *potential* subject-matter of moral judgment, for it strengthens or weakens some habit which influences whole classes of judgments."[14] And again, "potentially [moral] conduct is one hundred per cent of our conscious life. For all acts are so tied together that any one of them may have to be judged as an expression of character."[15]

One question which presents itself as a result of these considerations is: if all of our conduct is potentially moral in nature, how can parts of it be selected out and referred to as "moral situations"? The answer lies in Dewey's general view of the nature of doubt. A moral situation is characterized by doubt, by indecision. However, for Dewey, the notion of doubt is relative. As noted in the discussion of deliberation in Chapter Two, it is not possible to be in doubt about everything at once. To be in doubt about one thing is to take other things for granted.[16] In particular, it can be said that we are only able to recognize certain situations as moral situations or situations involving moral problems because situations which surround them are relatively settled. As Dewey notes, "many acts are done not only without thought of their *moral* quality but with practically no thought of any kind. Yet these acts are preconditions of other acts having significant value."[17] These "background" actions are for the most part composed of custom. As Dewey points out, "custom still forms the background of all moral life, nor can we imagine a state of affairs in which it should not. Customs are not external to individuals' courses of action; they are embodied in the habits and purposes of individuals...."[18]

In opposition to the actions we perform without thought (the customary or habitual actions) are the actions we are able to perform only after consideration of alternatives. The latter constitute the moral situations with which we are faced. Thus, for Dewey, "a moral situation is one in which judgment and choice are required antecedently to overt action. The practical meaning of the situation—that is to say the action needed to satisfy it—is not self-evident."[19]

Thus far a moral situation has been described as an occurrence which takes place more frequently than most would suppose, and that involves a judgment of better and worse. As such the characterization is still rather vague. Dewey makes the characteristics of a moral situation or problem more precise when he specifies that the choice demanded is one between competing values or goods. That is, contrary to common sense, a moral problem is not a choice between good and evil—or at least this is not the important sense of moral problem.[20] In the important sense of a moral problem, it is a choice "between values each of which is an undoubted good in its place but which now get in each other's way."[21] According to Dewey,

> all the serious perplexities of life come back to the genuine difficulty of forming a judgment as to the values of the situation; they come back to a conflict of goods. Only dogmatism can suppose that serious moral conflict is between something clearly bad and something known to be good, and that uncertainty lies wholly in the will of the one choosing. Most conflicts of importance are conflicts between things which are or have been satisfying, not between good and evil.[22]

More specifically, Dewey points out that moral problems may arise because of conflicting duties or loyalties,[23] or incompatible ideals or goals,[24] or because a nearby good is seen as conflicting with a far-off good.[25] The overall importance of each of these types of moral problems is that the individual, in choosing the one good over the other, is—by that same act—choosing to be one type of person rather than another.[26] That is, since the choice the individual makes will leave a permanent mark on that individual—affecting future choices—he/she is not merely deciding one individual preference, but setting in motion mechanisms of character and self which will continue indefinitely into future choices. As Dewey expresses the situation:

> This is the question finally at stake in any genuinely moral situation: What shall the agent *be?* What sort of character shall he assume? On its face, the question is what shall he do, shall he act for this or that end. But the incompatibility of the ends forces the issue back into the question of the kinds of selfhood, of agency, involved in the respective ends. The distinctively moral situation is then one in which elements of value and control are bound up with the processes of deliberation and desire; and are bound up in a peculiar way: *viz.,* they decide what kind of character shall control further desires and deliberations. When ends are genuinely incompatible, no common denominator can be found except by deciding what sort of character is most highly prized and shall be given supremacy.[27]

Summarizing these points concerning the nature of a moral situation, then, it can be said that for Dewey such a situation is marked by doubt arising from a felt conflict of values, ends, desires, duties, or priorities. The resolution of the doubt is given significance by the fact that the choice which will finally remove doubt in this situation will carry over into future situations and help control the very kinds of situations which will be recognized as having moral import in the future.

The study of the means by which ethical or moral problems are solved is called moral theory or ethics. The purpose of moral theory, according to Dewey, "is not to speculate upon man's final end and upon an ultimate standard of right, it is to utilize physiology, anthropology, and psychology to discover all that can be discovered of man, his organic powers and propensities."[28] Rather than dealing with human conduct in specific and segmented ways, as do the sciences mentioned above, ethics deals with conduct in its totality. It is an attempt to integrate all the elements in a situation which can render the final outcome intelligent. Thus Dewey says:

> This does not mean that it belongs to ethics to prescribe
> what man ought to do; but that its business is to detect
> the element of obligation in conduct, to examine con-
> duct to see what gives it its *worth*.... Ethics deals with
> conduct in its *entirety*, with reference, that is, to what
> makes it conduct, its end, its real meaning.[29]

From these comments it can be seen that moral theory, for Dewey, cannot itself settle moral problems. Moral theory does not arrive finally at specific right actions or a set of moral rules. Its goal is the more modest one of rendering personal choice more intelligent, not of taking the place of individual decision.[30]

To carry out this function of rendering moral choice more intelligent, Dewey believes that moral theory must pattern itself after the sciences through the adaptation of a scientific or logical problem solving method.[31] This is so for Dewey since "the value of any cognitive conclusion depends upon the *method* by which it is reached...."[32] The proper method in ethics, for Dewey, should be the method which has brought success to other areas of inquiry. Thus Dewey claims that "operational thinking needs to be applied to the judgment of values just as it has now finally been applied in conceptions of physical objects. Experimental empiricism in the field of ideas of good and bad is demanded to meet the conditions of the present situation."[33] In carrying through his reconstruction of ethical theory, Dewey revised and altered many traditional ethical notions. He began by distinguishing what he called customary morality from what he called reflective morality. Customary morality is involved in any situation where guidance of right and wrong is sought in tradition. In customary morality the past is the key to present conduct.[34] Reflective morality, on the other hand, begins with the belief that moral decisions are individual and a matter of personal choice. "Action," according to Dewey, "is always specific, concrete, individualized, unique. And consequently judgments as to acts to be performed must be similarly specific."[35] Further it demands that the standard used in making the personal choice be one of internal origin, of individual autonomy. For Dewey, "the essence of reflective morals is that it is conscious of the existence of a persistent self and of the part it plays in what is externally done."[36] Furthermore, "there can...be no such thing as reflective morality," according to Dewey, "except where men seriously ask by what purpose they should direct their conduct and why they should do so; what it is that makes their purposes good."[37]

2. The Context of the Moral Situation

The characterization of the moral situation given thus far is too general to give an accurate account of Dewey's position. One point which he stresses concerning such situations is that they involve deliberation and choice of better and worse; however, not every situation possessing the latter characteristics is properly called a moral situation. Dewey credits Aristotle with having set out the other considerations which narrow the concept of a moral situation. The first of these characteristics involves the agent knowing what he is about. That is, the agent must know and be able to understand the consequences and meanings of the various courses of action under consideration. Thus, presumably, a small child would be incapable of entering upon a moral situation.

The second characteristic demands merely that the agent who chooses a course of action intends to choose *that* course and is not somehow deluded in his/her choice. Finally, the third characteristic indicating that a situation of choice is truly a moral situation is that "the act must be the expression of a formed and stable *character,* in other words, the act must be *voluntary;* that is, it must manifest a choice, and for full morality at least, the choice must be an expression of the general tenor and set of personality."[38]

3. Desires and Ends-in-View

It was mentioned above that a moral situation occurs when an agent is presented with a choice of conflicting goods or values. If such is the case, the question naturally arises as to the nature of these goods, their source, and the source of their authority over our lives. In the discussion of Dewey's psychology in Chapter Two, it was asserted that desires arise in the course of our experience when something is felt as lacking—when for example, an impulse is not fulfilled, or a habit is frustrated. The situation marked by felt need and desire is one which calls for decision and resolution through action. The generic term Dewey uses to refer to the process involved in bringing such a situation to resolution is 'valuation.' 'Valuation' names the overall activity which begins with frustration and need and ends with overt activity to correct the situation. When it is recognized *what* is lacking in a situation, the individual experiences desire. Desire arises when the individual connects the felt frustration with the object which would, were it at hand, ameliorate the need. Dewey says of the process of valuation:

> Valuation takes place only when there is something the matter; when there is some trouble to be done away with, some need, lack, or privation to be made good, some conflict of tendencies to be resolved by means of changing existing conditions.[39]

The intellectual instrument used to bridge the gap between felt need and resolved situation is what Dewey calls an end-in-view. Ends-in-view are our conceptual projections—the intellectual tools through which we seek and find solutions for our problems. More specifically, an end-in-view for Dewey is the course of action which we hold up for examination, which, we hope, will bring a close to our frustration. Thus Dewey says, "an *end-in-view* arises when a particular consequence is foreseen and, being foreseen is consciously adopted by desire and deliberately made the directive purpose of action.[40] Further:

> An end-in-view thus differs on one side from a mere anticipation or prediction of an outcome, and on the other side, from the propulsive force of mere habit and appetite. In distinction from the first, it involves a want, an impulsive urge and forward drive; in distinction from the second, it involves an intellectual factor, the thought of an object which gives meaning and direction to the urge.[41]

To make the concept of ends-in-view clearer, it may be helpful to distinguish them from what they are not. Ends-in-view, for example, are not empty intellectual goals. They are not to be confused with what are called, in traditional ethical doctrine, "intrinsic goods," or "ends-in-themselves." Dewey is highly critical of the latter notion, for it gives no concrete pattern or guidance for action.[42] Ends-in-themselves, in the traditional theory, are things which are capable of value apart from the means of their attainment. Ends-in-view, on the other hand, must be tied in with means.[43] Thus Dewey says "it is simply impossible to have an end-in-view or to anticipate the consequences of any proposed line of action save upon the basis of some, however slight, consideration of the means by which it can be brought into existence."[44] Also, an end-in-view differs from an intrinsic good because the former involves "foreseen consequences which influence present deliberation and which finally bring it to rest by furnishing an adequate stimulus to overt action."[45] Ends-in-themselves (intrinsic goods) do not have these traits. They are thought of as ideals regardless of any individual's ability or desire to attain them.

Ends-in-view are also not mere mental states. For Dewey, "an end, aim or purpose as a *mental* state *is* independent of the biological and physical means by which it can be realized."[46] Ends-in-view, in contrast, directly involve an appreciation of means. Further, as a mental state, an end may not be personally attractive to us, whereas an end-in-view is always connected with a desire on our part.[47] "The mere conception of an end," according to Dewey, "is partly intellectual; there is nothing in it to move to action. It must be *felt* as valuable, as worth having, and as more valuable than the present condition before it can induct to action."[48]

Thus for Dewey a valuation is not intellectual in the sense of being a mental state—isolated from action. Valuations are understood in a behavioristic way by Dewey. The act of valuation is observable—it involves engaging the individual in some activity on the part of the thing valued. Thus Dewey says, "since desire and interest are behavioral phenomena (involving at the very least a 'motor' aspect), the valuations they produce are capable of being investigated as to their respective conditions and results. Valuations are empirically observable patterns of behavior and may be studied as such."[49]

While valuations cannot be "mere" intellectual or mental phenomena, they can also not be equated with simple attraction, desire, or interest. Although Dewey is emphatic that values must arise out of our desires, likings, and prizings, he is just as emphatic that not every thing we experience as a desire is worthy of being valued.[50] Thus he says "every person in the degree in which he is capable of learning from experience draws a distinction between what is desired and what is desirable whenever he engages in formation and choice of competing desires and interests."[51] The reason for this, according to Dewey, is that, "without intervention of thought, enjoyments are not values but problematic goods, becoming values when they reissue in a changed form from intelligent behavior."[52] And further, "enjoyments, objects of desire as they arise," for Dewey, "are *not* values, but are problematic material for construction—for creation if you will—of values."[53]

The difference between what is merely enjoyed or desired and what is determined to be enjoyable, desirable, is that while the former claim is a matter of empirical observation and personal history, the latter constitutes a prediction of probable consequences. The valuation which results in the belief that X is desirable, is a statement of anticipated results. It means, roughly, "When X is attained, the results will be favorable." Hence Dewey says

> to say that something is enjoyed is to make a statement
> about a fact...it is not to judge the value of the fact....
> But to call an object a value is to assert that it satisfies
> or fulfills certain conditions.[54]

Therefore, for Dewey, values involve both an intellectual and a biological or psychological aspect. The candidates for valuation are felt desires, but their election to the position of values—to ends-in-view worthy of guiding our actions—is a matter of intelligence. It is a matter, that is, of tracing the conditions and consequences of each proposed value to determine its larger contextual setting. Or, as Dewey points out, "the distinction is one between goods which, when they present themselves to imagination, are approved by reflection after wide examination of their relations, and the goods which are such only because their wider connections are not looked into."[55]

4. Conflicts of Ends and Intelligence

When the valuation process selects between two present desires, and proclaims that while both are just as truly desires only one is desirable, we have the basis of a moral decision. The need for a selection is forced by the fact that the two desires are somehow in conflict. If the basis of the conflict is serious enough that an individual's habits and thus his/her character stand to be affected by the choice, then it becomes genuinely a moral decision. Put another way, a moral decision does not arise with every choice between desires. If one chooses between a desire for rhubarb pie and a desire for banana cake, no moral situation is likely to arise. If the choice of one desire, however, has a tendency to strengthen a certain impulse at the expense of another and thus to develop one habit rather than another, then the conflict of desires has wider consequences—the choice will affect the individual's developing character. Accordingly, Dewey says:

> But let the value of one proposed end be felt to be really
> incompatible with that of another, let it be felt to be so

opposed as to appeal to a different kind of interest and choice, in other words, to different kinds of dispositions and agency, and we have a moral situation.[56]

This being the case, the problem becomes one of finding the best method of selecting what ought to be desired out of the field of things we may in fact experience as desires.

It is in this setting that Dewey finds the need for intelligence most critical. Thus he says, "the proper business of intelligence is discrimination of multiple and present goods and of the varied and immediate means of their realization; not search for the one remote aim."[57] He finds, however, that too often moral theorists have set their sights on discovering the "one remote aim" or set of immutable rules designed to settle all moral problems. Concerning the latter Dewey says:

> Ready-made rules available at a moment's notice for settling any kind of moral difficulty and resolving every species of moral doubt have been the chief object of the ambition of moralists. In the much less complicated and less changing matters of bodily health such pretensions are known as quackery. But in morals a hankering for certainty, born of timidity and nourished by love of authoritative prestige, has led to the idea that absence of immutability fixed and universally applicable ready-made principles is equivalent to moral chaos.[58]

The use of intelligence in morals means, for Dewey, that ends sought are ends-in-view rather than ends-in-themselves or final ends. Further, it means that the methods which have brought success to the sciences must be applied to morals.[59] The use of scientific methods, which by their nature dispense with final ends, will result, according to Dewey, in the quickening of

> inquiry into the diversity of specific goods of experience, fix attention upon their conditions, and bring to light values now dim and obscure. The change may relieve men from responsibility for what they cannot do, but it will promote thoughtful consideration of what they may do and the definition of responsibility for what they do amiss because of failure to think straight and carefully.[60]

In place of fixed rules and ends, Dewey's ethics calls for intelligent decision as to the best option available in the context of the situation. But for Dewey, the "best" in one situation is merely better than the other options—and thus the "better than" is the "good." Hence, as Dewey says:

> The better is the good; the best is not better than the good but is simply the discovered good. Comparative and superlative degrees are only paths to the positive degree of action. The worse or evil is a rejected good. In deliberation and before choice no evil presents itself as evil. Until it is rejected, it is a competing good. After rejection, it figures not as a lesser good, but as the bad of that situation.[61]

A corollary to these statements is Dewey's belief that what is best or the good in one situation need not be so in another situation; because of this, potentially any good can be improved upon in future situations. Thus, just as Dewey's view of truth entails that the truth is ever developing and being added to, so the good is always open to improvement. This view is known as "meliorism" and in general it involves the belief that "the specific conditions which exist at one moment, be they comparatively bad or comparatively good, in any event may be bettered."[62]

Drawing these last points together, then, it becomes clear that Dewey's ethics is based on the assumption that valuation is a natural process which involves the release of an individual from his/her desires through the projection of an end-in-view and the implementation in action of the means necessary to its fulfillment. The value of the end-in-view is measured experimentally by its success in releasing the individual from the desire in question. Though the process of valuation is involved in ethics, it is not the whole picture. Ethical theory deals with the resolution of moral problems. The latter are complex instances of valuation, wherein more than one desire is present at once, and the fulfillment of the specific desires in question is not possible because they conflict. Or, put another way, when an individual realizes that his/her problem is a moral problem, what he/she realizes is that the ends-in-view which he/she has projected at that point are mutually exclusive. They are such in the sense that the pursuit of one end-in-view will involve developing some aspect of character (or habit) which would be incompatible with the aspects of character which would be developed were he/she to pursue the other end-in-view. The choice in a moral problem, then, is really a choice of selves and what is required by ethical theory is an examination of the means open to the resolving of such problems.

To try to solve all moral problems by appealing to fixed rules, as in casuistry, is for Dewey, an impossibility.[63] In place of earlier ethical theories with their formulae for conduct, absolute rules, and fixed goals, Dewey proposes that intelligent moral decision making involves the use of a conscious moral deliberation. The deliberation is not different in kind from deliberation about other aspects of life. It is not assumed ahead of time that there is one transcendent good to be sought out, but that intelligent choice involves tracing the implications—that is determining the meaning—of the ends-in-view which are in conflict. Thus moral knowledge, like all knowledge for Dewey, consists in the meanings attached to various ways of acting. Thus Dewey says

> moral deliberation differs from other forms not as a process of forming a judgment and arriving at knowledge but in the kind of value which is thought about. The value is technical, professional, economic, etc., as long as one thinks of it as something one can aim at and attain by way of having, *possessing;* as something to be got or to be missed. Precisely the same object will have a moral value when it is thought of as making a difference in the *self,* as determining what one will *be,* instead of merely what one will have.[64]

The outcome of moral deliberation can be called the good, but it must be mentioned that for Dewey the good is "never twice alike" in quality.[65] Rather, he says, "good consists in the meaning that is experienced to belong to an activity when conflict and entanglement of various incompatible impulses and habits terminate in a unified orderly release in action."[66]

5. *The Goal of Moral Deliberation*

The process of moral deliberation is an intellectual as well as an emotional process for Dewey. Intellectually it consists in the imaginative tracing of courses of action and in the investigation of their likely consequences. In so doing we are evaluating the relative merits of various ends-in-view. However, this intellectual process would be of little significance, according to Dewey, were it not for the fact that as we proceed to feature to ourselves the ends-in-view and their meanings, we are aware of feelings which arise in us as we pass on different thoughts. Thus he says "the practical value of our acts is defined to us at any given time by the satisfaction, or displeasure, we take in the ideas of changes we foresee in case the act takes place."[67] The feelings which we experience as we sift through likely courses of action and their probable consequences are meaningful to us in the degree to which we assume that they will resemble the actual feelings we will experience when we act out our ideas. The arousal of such feelings do not of themselves settle the moral problem, for as sometimes happens we must pass judgment on the value and meaning of the feelings themselves. Thus Dewey says:

> We estimate the import or significance of any present desire or impulse by forecasting what it will come or amount to if carried out; literally its consequences define its *consequence*, its meaning or import. But if these consequences are conceived *merely as remote*, if their picturing does not arouse a present sense of peace, of fulfillment, or of dissatisfaction, of incompletion and irritation, the process of thinking out consequences remains purely intellectual.[68]

In forecasting the probable outcomes of different courses of action, Dewey suggests two measures of the adequacy of moral deliberation. The first, as he points out, is

> the adequacy with which inquiry into the lacks and conflicts of the existing situation has been carried on. The second is the adequacy of the inquiry into the likelihood that the particular end-in-view which is set up will, if acted upon, actually fill the existing need, satisfy the requirements constituted by what is needed, and do away with conflict by directing activity so as to institute a unified state of affairs.[69]

When it is seen that moral deliberation is not merely a process of settling a specific problem for the time being, but part of a larger process of character formation, it is a short step to the belief that "the educative process is all one with the moral process, since the latter is a continuous passage of experience from worse to better."[70] On this point Dewey states:

> When we observe that morals is at home whenever considerations of the worse and better are involved, we are committed to noting that morality is a continuing process not a fixed achievement. Morals means growth of conduct in meaning; at least it means that kind of expansion in meaning which is consequent upon observations of the conditions and outcome of conduct. It is all one with growing.... In the largest sense of the word, morals is education.[71]

For Dewey the belief that we may eventually become fully moral in our conduct is analogous to the belief that we may eventually become fully educated. Both beliefs are equally unwarranted. Concerning this latter point Dewey is emphatic that

> there is after all no such thing as complete moral maturity; all persons are still more or less children—in process of learning moral distinctions. The more intense their moral interests, the more childlike, the more open, flexible, and growing are their minds. It is only the callous and indifferent, or at least the conventional who find all acts and projects so definitely right and wrong as to render reflection unnecessary.[72]

In Dewey's ethical theory a dramatic shift is made relative to earlier ethical theories. While the latter constantly focus attention on actions and specific outcomes, Dewey focuses attention on the interaction which is constantly underway between the self, which is being created, and the individual's actions. Dewey's emphasis, in other words, is on the process involved in development, on the growth process. Hence, "the process of growth, of improvement and progress," for Dewey, "rather than the static outcome and result, becomes the significant thing."[73]

Rather than being concerned with specific acts, Dewey emphasizes the agent as a developing phenomenon. The questions to ask about a morally significant act must not all relate to its immediate and overt consequences. Rather, they must also assess the act's effects on the agent's character—and in particular on these effects as they bear on the agent's future growth. As Dewey notes: "Growth is the only moral 'end.'"[74] Because of this, the moral end can be viewed from a psychological perspective. In this sense, the problem of morality, according to Dewey,

is the formation, out of the body of original instinctive
impulses which compose the natural self, of a voluntary
self in which socialized desires and affections are dominant, and in which the last and controlling principle of
deliberation is the love of the objects which make this
transformation possible.[75]

As a result of these considerations it may be seen that the goal of moral
development (the general context in which specific moral situations are to
be dealt with) is growth and a growth which makes further growth possible.
If one begins with the psychology of the situation, Dewey's point is that
our impulses can be fulfilled in many ways (as mentioned in Chapter Two).
Because of this we have a choice of how they are to be fulfilled. The best
fulfillments will be those which open the individual up to new possibilities
and at the same time integrate with the similar fulfillment of other
impulses.

In the moral sphere this translates for Dewey as "the bad act is partial,
the good act organic."[76] Or put more completely:

The basis for discriminating between "right" and wrong
is found in the fact that some acts tend to narrow the self,
to introduce friction into it, to weaken its power, and in
various ways to *disintegrate* it, while other acts tend to
expand, invigorate, harmonize, and in general organize
the self.[77]

The statement "This act is right" can be analyzed as follows for
Dewey:

the subject, "this act," in the judgment "this act is right,"
is an act mediated by reference to the other experiences
it occasions—its effect upon the self. The predicate "is
right" simply traces out such effects more, completely,
taking into account, so far as possible, the reaction into
the future character of the self, and in virtue of this
reaction, judging the act.[78]

Put in general terms this means that

*the completest possible interaction of an impulse with
all other experiences, or the completest possible rela-*

tion of an impulse to the whole self constitutes the
predicate, or moral value, of an act.[79]

When this analysis is applied to the individual as a whole, it becomes clear that the individual's character is called good because of the integration of his/her impulses and the subsequent integration of interests, desires, and goals which compose his/her personality. For Dewey the rightness of actions is more basic than the goodness of character; the latter is dependent on the former. A good character, according to Dewey, is simply one which regularly performs right acts. In Dewey's words, "the good man . . . is his whole self in each of his acts; the bad man is partial (and hence a different) self in his conduct. He is not one person, for he has no unifying principle."[80]

6. Rules and Principles

Although Dewey, as mentioned above, was opposed to the idea of specific moral rules which are designed to apply absolutely to moral situations, he was not opposed to moral rules in general. The same may be said of moral principles. The two—rules and principles—are not the same, but mark off different degrees of specificity. On this Dewey says:

> *Rules are practical; they are habitual ways of doing things. But principles are intellectual; they are useful methods of judging things.... Whereas the object of moral principles is to supply standpoints and methods which will enable the individual to make for himself an analysis of the elements of good and evil and the particular situation in which he finds himself. No genuine moral principle prescribes a specific course of action....* [81]

And also he states that

> a genuine principle differs from a rule in two ways:
> (a) A principle evolves in connection with the course of experience, being a generalized statement of what sort of consequences and values tend to be realized in certain kinds of situations; a rule is taken as something ready-made and fixed.
> (b) A principle is primarily intellectual, a method and scheme for judging, and is practical secondarily because of what it discloses; a rule is primarily practical.[82]

According to Dewey, rules and principles are most helpful in moral deliberation when they are used as hypotheses. This was part of Dewey's program for making ethical theory more scientific. Accordingly, he points out that:

> A... significant change that would issue from carrying over experimental method from physics to man concerns the import of standards, principles, rules. With the transfer, these, and *all* tenets and creeds about good and goods, would be recognized to be hypotheses. Instead of being rigidly fixed, they would be treated as intellectual instruments to be tested and confirmed—and altered—through consequences effected by acting upon them.[83]

The use of rules and principles as hypotheses has the following effect, according to Dewey: "Rules are softened into principles, and principles are modified into methods of understanding."[84] Thus rules and principles used as hypotheses would aid moral deliberation by encouraging it to remain experimental and flexible. But like all hypotheses, the moral rules and principles in question would always be open to revision in light of the results which their use brought about. Further, using rules and principles as hypotheses opens up the past history of their use as a resource in present deliberation. We are not committed to repeating the errors of the past. Rather we can look at the use made of specific principles under specific conditions in the past, and note the results. On this Dewey says, "principles exist as hypotheses with which to experiment. Human history is long. There is a long record of past experimentation in conduct, and there are cumulative verifications which give many principles a well earned prestige."[85]

7. Duty

Dewey's view of duty arises from his concept of the purpose of moral deliberation and his concept of right conduct. If moral deliberation has as its goal the unification of the personality or the self, then duty must be a response to this ideal. If right actions are those which, better than other alternatives, give vent to impulses in ways which help to integrate all impulses, then too, duty must be a response to this demand. On the other hand, according to Dewey,

a man's duty is never to obey certain rules; his duty
is always to respond to the nature of the actual
demands which he finds made upon him,—demands
which do not proceed from abstract rules, nor from
ideals however awe-inspiring and exalted, but from
the concrete relations to men and things in which he
finds himself.[86]

Rather, he says:

Duty is what is owed by a partial isolated self embodied in established, facile, and urgent tendencies, to
that ideal self which is presented in aspirations
which, since they are not yet formed into habits, have
no organized hold upon the self and which can get
organized into habitual tendencies and interests only
by a more or less painful and difficult reconstruction
of the habitual self.[87]

Further, for Dewey, duty is an emergent phenomenon. It is not
something which a child can yet have, for "a self without habits, one loose
and fluid, in which change in one direction is just as easy as in another,
would not have the sense of duty."[88] Duty only gradually emerges as the
self begins to stabilize and form strong habits.

On the other hand, duty requires a flexibility of self. "A self with no
new possibilities, rigidly set in conditions and perfectly accommodated to
them, would not have it."[89] Consequently, duty arises only in individuals
capable of moral deliberation—that is in individuals capable of recognizing moral situations. The ingredients of such a situation include, for
Dewey,

definite, persistent, urgent tendencies to act in a given
way, occurring at the same time with other incompatible
tendencies which represent the self more adequately
and yet are not organized into habits.... [90]

Duty, therefore, is simply another side of the moral situation. It is that
situation seen from the perspective of the self choosing its direction of
growth, and experiencing the tension born of conflict.

8. Virtue and Sympathy

To this point in the discussion of Dewey's ethics, consideration has been almost exclusively concerned with the individual and his/her personal moral growth as grounded in individual psychological dynamics. Little has been said, therefore, concerning the place of social interrelations in Dewey's ethics.

The positive ways in which an individual can relate and interact with others are called virtues. Of these Dewey says, "the habits of character whose effect is to sustain and spread the rational or common good are virtues; the traits of character which have the opposite effect are vices."[91] More specifically, he defines virtue in the following way:

> A virtue may be defined... either as *the settled intelligent identification of an agent's capacity with some aspect of the reasonable or common happiness;* or, *as a social custom or tendency organized into a personal habit of valuation.* From the latter standpoint, truthfulness is the social institution of language maintained at its best pitch of efficiency through the habitual purposes of individuals; from the former, it is an instinctive capacity and tendency to communicate emotions and ideas directed so as to maintain social peace and prosperity.[92]

Though Dewey's entire ethical theory is permeated by the premise that what is open to experiment, observation, and control is more useful than what is private and inaccessible, the behavioristic tone of his ethics is most evident in his discussion of virtue. This is the case for Dewey, since virtuous conduct, as he understands it, has certain observable characteristics. That conduct is virtuous does not depend for Dewey, as it has for many earlier moral theorists, on the existence of certain private feelings or intentions in the "mind" of the agent. While such feelings or intentions may well exist in cases of conduct called virtuous, they are not the determining factor in their being called virtuous. Rather, virtuous acts are determined on an outward observable basis. Hence Dewey says:

> Honesty, chastity, malice, peevishness, courage, triviality, industry, irresponsibility are not private possessions of a person. They are working adaptations of

personal capacities with environing forces. All virtues and vices are habits which incorporate objective forces. They are interactions of elements contributed by the make-up of an individual with elements supplied by the outdoor world. They can be studied objectively as physiological functions, and they can be modified by change of either personal or social elements.[93]

Of all the virtues, it is sympathy which holds the most important position for Dewey, not merely because, as he believes, it has its basis directly in our biological/ genetic make-up, but because it is central to the other virtues, being their foundation and basis.

Dewey's strongest statements on the significance of sympathy came in his early work *Psychology* (1887). These statements were later modified to some extent. However, since sympathy plays a central role in the social aspect of Dewey's ethical theory, the development of his concept of sympathy is worthy of some consideration at this point.

Dewey's discussion of sympathy in his *Psychology* comes within a section concerned with feelings in general and social feelings in particular. The latter, according to Dewey, give rise to what he calls "moral feelings." In a moral feeling, for Dewey,

> the sense of rightness, the feeling of the harmony existing between an act of a person and the ideal — that is, the perfectly objective and universal — personality is realized; the feeling of the wrongness of an act is the feeling that it does not conform to this ideal of personality, but contravenes it.[94]

In speaking of "the perfectly objective and universal personality" Dewey reveals the idealistic attachment he still maintained at this point. This idealistic influence is more patent in the following statement where Dewey contrasts moral feelings with social feelings:

> The essence of social feeling is that in it man feels himself identified with a self more comprehensive, more permanent than his own private and particular being. He feels his true life to be that of all personalities; he feels, in short, that he cannot realize himself except in a self which will unite and harmonize all the varied experiences of humanity. It is not meant, of course, that

this relation of the actual self to the ideal, universal self is consciously recognized by all to be present when they experience social feeling. It is only meant that a fair analysis reveals this relation as constituting its essence. But in moral feeling this relation is brought more explicitly into consciousness. In moral feeling man feels his true self to be one which comprehends possible relations to all men, and all acts which are necessary to bring the actual self into harmony with this true self, to make his will, in other words, conform to a universal will, he conceives as *duties*.[95]

The source of moral feeling, for Dewey, is the feeling of sympathy; it makes the moral feeling possible.[96] This is the case, for Dewey, since in feeling sympathy it is as if we are "feeling someone else's feelings." Thus he says, "this feeling [sympathy] results from an identification with self of such experience of others as are felt to be possible experiences of our own."[97] The basis of sympathy, according to Dewey, is found in the tendency to imitate others. Thus he says:

> Sympathy has its origin in what is termed resonance or contagion of feeling. There is a psychical atmosphere as well as a physical, and one living in this atmosphere absorbs and reflects it. Laughter and crying are both "catching." We unconsciously reproduce the feelings of those about us; we take on their mood unaware.[98]

In Dewey's early view, the function of sympathy in human interrelations (and hence in ethics) cannot be over emphasized. "Sympathy," Dewey says, "is the bond of union between men; it is to the social sphere what gravitation is to the physical."[99] Further, for Dewey, "sympathy is the sole means by which persons come within the range of our life. It is thus an extremely universal feeling, for it takes us beyond what constitutes our immediate personality, our private interests and concerns, into what universally constitutes personality."[100]

From these remarks it can be seen that in Dewey's early view, sympathy forms a link between ethics and human psychology at two points. On the one hand, the purely moral feeling of rightness, for example, is traceable to, but evidently not reducible to, sympathy, which in turn has its origin in organic activities of the individual. Going in the other direction, however, the moral feelings lead to or culminate in the psychological process of personality development. Sympathy stands, therefore, as a step between organic processes which lead to it, and the developing personality, to which it gives rise. In his later writings, Dewey continued to emphasize the moral significance of sympathy. Thus in the 1908 *Ethics,* for example, he states that "it is sympathy transformed into a habitual standpoint which satisfies the demand for a standpoint which will render the person interested in foresight of all obscure consequences."[101] And further:

> It is sympathy which carries thought out beyond the self and which extends its scope till it approaches the universal as its limit. It is sympathy which saves consideration of consequences from degenerating into mere calculation, by rendering vivid the interests of others and urging us to give them the same weight as those which touch our own honor, purse, and power. To put ourselves in the place of others, to see things from the standpoint of their purposes and values, to humble, contrariwise, our own pretensions and claims till they reach the level they would assume in the eye of an impartial sympathetic observer, is the surest way to attain objectivity of moral knowledge. Sympathy is the animating mold of moral judgment not because its dictates take precedence in action over those of other impulses (which they do not do), but because it furnishes the most efficacious *intellectual* standpoint. It is the tool, *par excellence,* for resolving complex situations.[102]

It can be seen in this last quotation that the goal, sympathy, had changed from Dewey's view expressed in the *Psychology* to his later writings; though Dewey's view of the importance of sympathy for the moral life was quite consistent. His early view presented sympathy as leading, potentially, to a universal personality. That is, Dewey's early view, with its idealistic underpinnings, apparently held the growth of personality to be progressing toward an ideal in the sense of an abstract universal. The universal personality, for Dewey, was the element common to all individual personalities—as a transcendent unity. In his later view, however, the goal of sympathy is a hypothetical viewpoint—the sympathy of an ideal impartial observer. The latter ideal is one we construct for ourselves, the former is an antecedent existent.

Although Dewey believes sympathy to be invaluable for moral deliberation, he is not unaware of its potential evils, especially in his later writings. One of these evils or limitations lies in the fact that sympathy may be restricted in its scope. We may be led to picking and choosing with whom we are to sympathize. Accordingly, Dewey says:

> There are, however, definite limitations to the spontaneous and customary exercise of sympathetic admiration and resentment. It rarely extends beyond those near to us, members of our own family and our friends. It rarely operates with reference to those out of sight or to strangers certainly not to enemies.[103]

In addition, he realizes that as a raw urge or impulse, sympathy may become the basis of many sorts of actions of different moral value.[104] To serve as the supreme tool of moral deliberation, sympathy is something that must be guided and cultivated by the social environment.[105]

Contrasting the moral quality or virtue of sympathy with its original appearance as a biological endowment of the individual, Dewey says

> a genuine social interest is then something much broader and deeper than an instinctive sympathetic reaction. Sympathy is a genuine natural instinct, varying in intensity in different individuals. It is a precious instrumentality for the development of social insight and socialized affection; but in and of itself it is upon the same plane as any natural endowment. It may lead to sentimentality or to selfishness; the individual may shrink from scenes of misery just because of the pain they cause him, or may seek jovial companions because of the sympathetic pleasures he gets.... Again instinctive sympathy is partial; it may attach itself vehemently to those of blood kin or to immediate associates in such a way as to favor them at the expense of others, and lead to positive injustice toward those beyond the charmed circle.[106]

9. Ethics and Psychology

In this chapter the main points of Dewey's ethical theory have been set forth. The significant point which lay behind their exposition here is the fact that Dewey was not content merely to generate a logically consistent or intuitively appealing ethical position, but at every point was concerned to seek a psychological basis for his views. Only by so doing could he insure that its prescriptive elements were in line with, and grew out of, an individual's impulses, habits, desires—that is, human nature.

In addition, it should be seen that what Dewey used as the psychological foundation for his ethics was never the speculation of an introspective psychologist, but rather, the outward measurable aspects of conduct. As a result, his ethical theory is free from hints of purely "mental" phenomena operating in the moral sphere. Each of the important concepts in his ethics, from intelligence to sympathy, from deliberation to moral growth, can and have been given a description such that it is the whole individual who is involved in the moral life. Put another way, because the key concepts in his ethical theory can be given operational or behavioral significance, Dewey at no time is pressed to fall back upon an inner autonomous "moral agent" or use the concepts of moral intuition or moral sense. These advances in ethical theory can be attributed, to a great extent, to his insistence on a behavioristic psychology as the basis for his ethics. And, as will be brought out in Chapter Five, the combination of a naturalistic ethic and a behavioristic psychology presents the factors required for the effective control of our behavior and a basis for the initiating of such control toward specific aims.

Before that discussion, however, Dewey's views on ethics and psychology will be compared with those of B. F. Skinner. By comparing the views of Dewey and Skinner, it should become possible to see what aspects of Dewey's moral theory are rendered necessary by his acceptance of a behavioristic psychology, and which aspects had an independent origin. In addition it will be possible to isolate specific differences between the behavioristic psychologies of Dewey and Skinner and to assess the significance of these differences for moral theory.

Endnotes

[1] Dewey, *Problems of Men*, p. 239.

[2] Ibid.

[3] Dewey, *Theory of Valuation*, pp. 62-63.

[4] Dewey, *Human Nature and Conduct*, p. 86. Dewey also says, "Beliefs about values are pretty much in the position in which beliefs about nature were before the scientific revolution" (The *Quest for Certainty*, p. 256).

[5] Dewey, "Experience, Knowledge and Value," p. 526.

[6] Dewey says "ethical theory arises from practical needs, and is not simply a judgment about conduct, but a part of conduct, a practical fact" (*The Study of Ethics: A Syllabus*, p. 225).

[7] Dewey and Tufts, *Ethics* (1932), p. 343.

[8] Ibid., p. 344.

[9] Dewey and Tufts, *Ethics* (1908), p. 212.

[10] Dewey, *Outlines of a Critical Theory of Ethics*, p. 2. See also, Dewey, *The Study of Ethics: A Syllabus*, p. 224.

[11] Dewey, *Human Nature and Conduct*, p. 278.

[12] Dewey and Tufts, *Ethics* (1932), p. 179. Dewey also notes, "we feel that it would be rather morbid if a moral issue were raised in connection with each act; we should probably suspect some mental disorder if it were, at least some weakness in power of decision" (Ibid., p. 178).

[13] Dewey, *Human Nature and Conduct*, p. 281.

[14] Dewey and Tufts, *Ethics* (1908), p. 211.

[15] Dewey and Tufts, *Ethics* (1932), p. 180.

[16] Dewey, *Logic*, p. 108.

[17] Dewey and Tufts, *Ethics* (1932), p. 178.

[18] Dewey and Tufts, *Ethics* (1908), p. 332.

[19] Dewey, *Reconstruction in Philosophy*, p. 163.

[20] Dewey and Tufts, *Ethics* (1932), p. 174.

[21] Ibid.

[22] Dewey, *The Quest for Certainty*, p. 266.

[23] Dewey and Tufts, *Ethics* (1932), p. 174.

[24] Dewey and Tufts, *Ethics* (1908), p. 207.

[25] Dewey and Tufts, *Ethics* (1932), p. 200.

[26] Dewey, *The Study of Ethics: A Syllabus*, p. 224.

[27] Dewey and Tufts, *Ethics* (1908), p. 210. See also, Dewey and Tufts, *Ethics (1932)*, pp. 302 and 317.

[28] Dewey, *The Influence of Darwin on Philosophy*, p. 69.

[29] Dewey, *Outlines of a Critical Theory of Ethics*, p. 1.

[30] Dewey and Tufts, *Ethics* (1932), p. 176.

[31] Dewey, *Reconstruction in Philosophy*, p. 73.

[32] Dewey, *The Quest for Certainty*, p. 200.

[33] Ibid., p. 258.

[34] Dewey and Tufts, *Ethics* (1932), p. 171.

[35] Dewey, *Reconstruction in Philosophy*, p. 167.

[36] Dewey and Tufts, *Ethics* (1932), p. 183.

[37] Ibid., pp. 197-198.

[38] Ibid., p. 176. See also, Dewey, *The Study of Ethics: A Syllabus*, p. 240.

[39] Dewey, *Theory of Valuation*, p. 34.

[40] Dewey and Tufts, *Ethics* (1939), p. 199.

[41] Ibid.

[42] Dewey, *Reconstruction in Philosophy*, p. 170.

[43] Dewey states:

> Ends are appraised in the same evaluation in which things as means are weighed. For example, an end suggests itself. But when things are weighed as means toward that end, it is found that it will take too much time or too great an expenditure of energy to achieve it, or that, if it were attained, it would bring with it certain accompanying inconveniences and the promise of future troubles. It is then appraised and rejected as a 'bad' end *(Theory of Valuation*, p. 24).

[44] Ibid., p. 35.

[45] Dewey, *Human Nature and Conduct*, p. 223.

[46] Dewey, *Theory of Valuation*, p. 36.

[47] Dewey and Tufts, *Ethics* (1932), p. 269.

[48] Dewey, *Outlines of a Critical Theory of Ethics*, p. 85.

[49] Dewey, *Theory of Valuation*, p. 51.

[50] Dewey and Tufts, *Ethics* (1932), p. 206. See also, Dewey, *The Quest for Certainty*, p. 264.

[51] Dewey, *Theory of Valuation*, p. 31

[52] Dewey, *The Quest for Certainty*, p. 259.

[53] Dewey, "Experience, Knowledge and Value," p. 583.

[54] Dewey, *The Quest for Certainty*, p. 260.

[55] Dewey and Tufts, *Ethics* (1932), p. 229.

[56] Dewey and Tufts, *Ethics* (1908), p. 207.

[57] Dewey, *The Influence of Darwin on Philosophy*, pp. 67-68.

[58] Dewey, *Human Nature and Conduct*, p. 238.

[59] Dewey, *Reconstruction in Philosophy* (1948), p. xiii.

[60] Dewey, *The Influence of Darwin on Philosophy*, pp. 70-71.

[61] Dewey, *Human Nature and Conduct*, p. 278.

[62] Dewey, *Reconstruction in Philosophy*, p. 178.

[63] Dewey, *The Study of Ethics: A Syllabus*, p. 226.

[64] Dewey and Tufts, *Ethics* (1932), p. 302.

[65] Dewey, *Human Nature and Conduct*, p. 211.

[66] Ibid., p. 210.

[67] Dewey and Tufts, *Ethics* (1908), p. 278.

[68] Dewey and Tufts, *Ethics* (1932), pp. 302-303.

[69] Dewey, *Theory of Valuation*, pp. 34-35.

[70] Dewey, *Reconstruction in Philosophy*, p. 183.

[71] Dewey, *Human Nature and Conduct*, p. 280.

[72] Dewey and Tufts, *Ethics* (1908), pp. 320-321.

[73] Dewey, *Reconstruction in Philosophy*, p. 177.

[74] Ibid.

[75] Dewey and Tufts, *Ethics* (1908), p. 397.

[76] Dewey, *The Study of Ethics: A Syllabus*, p. 245.

[77] Ibid., p. 244.

[78] Ibid.

[79] Ibid.

[80] Ibid., p. 245.

[81] Dewey and Tufts, *Ethics* (1908), p. 333; Cf. Dewey and Tufts, *Ethics* (1932), p. 309.

[82] Dewey and Tufts, *Ethics* (1932), pp. 304-305.

[83] Dewey, *The Quest for Certainty*, p. 277.

[84] Dewey, *Reconstruction in Philosophy*, p. 161.

[85] Dewey, *Human Nature and Conduct*, p. 239.

[86] Dewey, "Moral Theory and Practice," *International Journal of Ethics* 1 (Jan. 1891); reprinted in *The Early Works of John Dewey, 1882-1898*, George E. Axtelle, et al., eds., 5 vols. (Carbondale and Edwardsville: Southern Illinois University Press, 1969), 3:106.

[87] Dewey and Tufts, *Ethics* (1908), p. 362.

[88] Ibid., p. 343.

[89] Ibid.

[90] Ibid.

[91] Ibid., p. 399.

[92] Ibid., p. 403.

[93] Dewey, *Human Nature and Conduct*, p. 16.

[94] Dewey, *Psychology*, pp. 288-289.

[95] Ibid., p. 289.

[96] Ibid., p. 288.

[97] Ibid., p. 283.

[98] Ibid., p. 284.

[99] Ibid., p. 286.

[100] Ibid., pp. 285-286.

[101] Dewey and Tufts, *Ethics* (1908), p. 300.

[102] Dewey and Tufts, *Ethics* (1932), pp. 297-298. See also, Dewey and Tufts, *Ethics* (1908), p. 299.

[103] Dewey and Tufts, *Ethics* (1932), p. 261.

[104] Dewey and Tufts, *Ethics* (1908), p. 251.

[105] Dewey notes that

the emotion of sympathy is morally invaluable. But it functions properly when used as a principle of reflection and insight, rather than of direct action. Intelligent sympathy widens and deepens concern for consequences. To put ourselves in place of another, to see things from the standpoint of his aims and values, to humble our estimate of our pretensions to the levels they assume in the eyes of an impartial observer, is the surest way to appreciate what justice demands in concrete "cases" (Dewey and Tufts, *Ethics* [1932], p. 275).

[106] Dewey and Tufts, *Ethics* (1908), pp. 298-299.

SKINNER'S PSYCHOLOGY AND ITS RELATION TO ETHICS

Skinner, like Dewey, is impressed with the extent to which people living in a scientific age have carefully resisted the application of scientific principles to their own behavior. But, according to Skinner, "men have suffered long enough from that strange quirk in their behavior which keeps them from applying the methods of natural science to their own lives."[1] In part this "quirk" has resulted from the complexity of human behavior, combined with the "quest for certainty," that reveals itself as the desire felt by many people to believe something (even if it is false) rather than to be in doubt. Accordingly Skinner says

> behavior has that kind of complexity or intricacy which discourages simple description and in which magical explanatory concepts flourish abundantly. Primitive systems of behavior first set the pattern by placing the behavior of man under the direction of entities beyond man himself.... In more advanced systems of behavior, the ultimate direction and control have been assigned to entities placed within the organism and called psychic or mental. Nothing is gained by this stratagem because most, if not all, of the determinative properties of the original behavior must be assigned to the inner entity, which becomes, as it were, an organism in its own right.[2]

Thus, for Skinner, what have passed as attempts to give a scientific account of human behavior have actually been mere refinements of prescientific forms of explanation. All attempts to explain behavior in terms of inner agencies, faculties, or other mental constructs are referred to by Skinner as forms of "mentalism," and all as equally ineffective. Hence Skinner points out, "a pure mentalism has dominated Western thinking for more than two thousand years. Almost all versions contend that the mind is a nonphysical space in which events obey nonphysical laws."[3] And further, according to Skinner,

> mentalistic theories are subject to changes in fashion and, as in the history of clothing or architecture, one has only to wait long enough to find an earlier view back in style. We have had Aristotelian revivals and are now said to be returning to Plato. Modern psychology can claim to be far beyond Plato in controlling the environments of which people are said to be conscious, but it has not greatly improved their access to consciousness itself, because it has not been able to improve the verbal contingencies under which feelings and states of mind are described and known.[4]

The problem with mentalistic explanations, however, is not primarily that they introduce "nonphysical laws," or that they posit "nonphysical space," nor even that they are subject to changing fashions. Rather, the central problem with mentalistic explanations is that they give the pretense of accounting for psychological phenomena without at the same time giving access to effective prediction and control of behavior. Hence, as Skinner points out:

> The practice of looking inside the organism for an explanation of behavior has tended to obscure the variables which are immediately available for a scientific analysis. These variables lie outside the organism, in its immediate environment and in its environmental history. They have a physical status to which the usual techniques of science are adapted, and they make it possible to explain behavior as other subjects are explained in science.[5]

Thus, it should be noticed, Skinner does not deny the existence of mental events, instead, merely questions their usefulness as sources of explanation.[6] Hence, "the objection to inner states is not," says Skinner, "that they do not exist, but that they are not relevant in a functional analysis. We cannot account for the behavior of any system while staying wholly inside it; eventually we must turn to forces operating upon the organism from without."[7] As an illustration of this difficulty Skinner presents the following example. He asks:

> To what extent is it helpful to be told, "He drinks because he is thirsty"? If to be thirsty means nothing more than to have a tendency to drink, this is mere redundancy. If it means that he drinks because of a state of thirst, an inner causal event is evoked. If this state is purely inferential—if no dimensions are assigned to it which would make direct observation possible—it cannot serve as an explanation.[8]

As an antidote to what he considers the infelicitous mentalistic explanations to which we have become accustomed, Skinner, like Dewey, proposes that we adhere strictly to the examples of the physical sciences. Thus he states that "we need to go beyond mere observation to a study of functional relationships. We need to establish laws by virtue of which we may predict behavior and we may do this only by finding variables of which behavior is a function."[9] Skinner's point here is similar to that made by Dewey in *The Quest for Certainty,* and noted in Chapter One. The point concerns the fact that when the sciences have made progress it is because they have gone beyond the immediate qualities of the phenomena under study. Skinner amplifies this point when he says

> chemistry made great strides when it was recognized that the weights of combining substances, rather than their qualities or essences, were the important thing to study. The science of mechanics moved forward rapidly when it was discovered that distances and times were more important for certain purposes than size, shape, color, hardness, and weight. Many different properties or aspects of behavior have been studied for many years with varying degrees of success. A functional analysis which specifies behavior as a dependent variable and proposes to account for it in terms of observable and manipulable physical conditions is of recent advent. It has already shown itself to be a promising formulation,

and until it has been put to the test, we have no reason
to prophesy failure.[10]

Skinner finds, however, that many people do prophesy failure for the
type of analysis of behavior in which he is interested. "When a science of
behavior reaches the point of dealing with lawful relationships," says
Skinner, "it meets the resistance of those who give their allegiance to
prescientific or extrascientific conceptions."[11] This resistance and its
accompanying pessimism seem to be due, at least in part, to a realization
of some of the implications of a Skinnerian analysis of behavior. Among
these implications are a strict determinism, a denial of autonomous self-
caused activity, and a denial of ultimate human responsibility. On this
Skinner says:

> As a science of behavior adopts the strategy of physics
> and biology, the autonomous agent to which behavior
> has traditionally been attributed is replaced by the
> environment—the environment in which the species
> evolved and in which the behavior of the individual is
> shaped and maintained.[12]

And further:

> Science is more than the mere description of events as
> they occur. It is the attempt to discover order, to show
> that certain events stand in lawful relations to other
> events. No practical technology can be based upon
> science until such relations have been discovered.... If
> we are to use the methods of science in the field of
> human affairs, we must assume that behavior is lawful
> and determined. We must expect to discover that what
> a man does is the result of specifiable conditions and
> that once these conditions have been discovered, we can
> anticipate and to some extent determine his actions.[13]

The program of Skinner's psychology is, then, to attempt to account
for behavior through reference to external observable factors. How his
form of behaviorism differs from the earlier form of behaviorism, put forth
by Watson, will be explained in the final section of this chapter. In general
terms, Skinner outlines the procedures of his own behaviorism as follows:
"We want to know why men behave as they do. Any condition or event

which can be shown to have an effect upon behavior must be taken into account. By discovering and analyzing these causes we can predict behavior; to the extent that we can manipulate them, we can control behavior."[14]

1. Organism and Environment

Like Dewey, Skinner begins his psychological analysis with the behavior an organism manifests as a result of its interaction with its environment. The environment, and the history of an organism's interactions with the environment, form the context of Skinner's psychological perspective.

For Skinner there are two basic ways in which an organism can or does interact with its environment. Either the organism can adjust its behavior to the demands of the environment, or the organism can adjust the environment to its needs. In Dewey's writings two similar modes of organism-environment adjustment occur. Dewey calls the adjustment of the organism to the environment accommodation, and the adjustment of the environment by the organism adaptation. Concerning the former Dewey says:

> There are conditions we meet that cannot be changed. If they are particular and limited, we modify our own particular attitudes in accordance with them. Thus we accommodate ourselves to changes in weather, to alterations in income when we have no other recourse.... The two main traits of this attitude, which I should like to call accommodation, are that it affects *particular* modes of conduct, not the entire self, and that the process is mainly *passive*.[15]

Concerning adaptation Dewey says:

> A house is rebuilt to suit changed conditions of the household; the telephone is invented to serve the demand for speedy communication at a distance; dry soils are irrigated so that they may bear abundant crops. Instead of accommodating ourselves to conditions, we modify conditions so that they will be accommodated to our wants and purposes. This process may be called adaptation.[16]

Although Dewey's accommodation and adaptation are similar in general description to Skinner's respondent and operant behavior respectively, they are by no means the same in detail. Respondent behavior, or the organism's behavior which is elicited in *response* to the environment, begins with unconditioned reflexes. Many of these unconditioned reflexes "are executed by the 'smooth muscles' and the glands." According to Skinner, "these structures are particularly concerned with the internal economy of the organism."[17] Further, Skinner points out, "reflexes and other innate patterns of behavior evolve because they increase the chances of survival of the species."[18]

In a typical case of respondent behavior, an unconditioned stimulus in the environment elicits an unconditioned response in the organism. Thus a bright flash of light, for example, elicits the unconditioned response of pupil contraction. For respondent, or classical, or Pavlovian, conditioning to occur, the unconditioned stimulus must be paired with a previously neutral event. As the neutral event occurs in temporal proximity to the occurrence of the unconditioned stimulus, it too gains the property of eliciting the response in question. Thus the bright flash light, after numerous pairings with a certain tone, will condition a response to the tone itself. The tone henceforth will produce the pupillary reflex.

Though respondent behavior does occur and is important in explaining some behaviors in an organism, it no longer plays the major role in behavioristic analysis which it once did. Hence, Skinner says

> all conditioned reflexes are...based upon unconditioned reflexes. But we have seen that reflex responses are only a small part of the total behavior of the organism. Conditioning adds new controlling stimuli, but not new responses. In using the principle, therefore, we are not subscribing to a "conditioned-reflex" theory of all behavior.[19]

The importance once accorded to reflexes in a behavioristic analysis of behavior is now bestowed on the concept of operant behavior with its two forms: operant conditioning and operant discrimination. Operant behavior is characterized by the organism's *operating* on the environment, and the environment's responding in some way. The increased importance of operant behavior and the decreased importance of respondent behavior are due, in part at least, to the fact that respondent behavior is largely made up of what are usually called our involuntary actions, whereas operant behavior is composed primarily of what are called our voluntary acts.

In general terms operant behavior is that class of actions (called operants) which tend to increase or decrease in frequency depending on their consequences. Some operants lead to environmental reactions which tend to increase the frequency of the specific operant; others lead to environmental reactions which tend to decrease the frequency of the operant. Concerning operant behavior, Skinner says:

> There is a large body of behavior that does not seem to be *elicited*, in the sense in which a cinder in the eye elicits closure of the lid, although it may eventually stand in a different kind of relation to external stimuli. The original "spontaneous" activity of the organism is chiefly of this sort, as is the greater part of the conditioned behavior of the adult organism."[20]

In the above quotation it should be noted that what Skinner refers to as the "original 'spontaneous' activity of the organism" covers the same ground as Dewey's impulsion-impulse conceptual matrix. For Skinner operants are emitted by the organism rather than elicited by the environment. Depending on the result with which each operant is met it tends to increase or decrease in frequency. It will be recalled from Chapter Two, that, according to Dewey, the organism initially has impulsions which can develop into impulses. During the organism's history these impulses become modified because of their consequences, and in time may form the basis of habits.

Specifying further the nature of operant behavior, Skinner says

> operant behavior is simply a study of what used to be dealt with by the concept of purpose. The purpose of an act is the consequences it is going to have. Actually, in the case of operant conditioning, we study the consequences an act has had in the past. Changes in the probability of response are brought about when an act is followed by a particular kind of consequence.[21]

Operant behavior begins with an operant which is emitted by the organism and then followed by environmental consequences.[22] As the environmental consequences tend to increase or decrease the frequency of the operant, operant conditioning is said to take place. Concerning the latter, Skinner says:

> Operant conditioning can be described without men-
> tioning any stimulus which acts before the response is
> made.... Stimuli are always acting upon an organism,
> but their functional connection with operant behavior is
> not like that in a reflex. Operant behavior, in short, is
> *emitted,* rather than *elicited.* It must have this property
> if the notion of probability of response is to make
> sense.[23]

Without due caution it is easy to mistake the nature of operant
conditioning and assume that an organism performs an act or refrains from
so doing because of expected consequences. Accordingly, Skinner says:
"Instead of saying that a man behaves because of the consequences which
are to follow his behavior, we simply say that he behaves because of the
consequences which *have* followed similar behavior in the past."[24]

An environmental event which follows an operant and tends to
increase the frequency of that operant is said to be a reinforcer. As Skinner
points out,

> the only defining characteristic of a reinforcing stimu-
> lus is that it reinforces.
>
> The only way to tell whether or not a given event is
> reinforcing to a given organism under given conditions
> is to make a direct test. We observe the frequency of a
> selected response, then make an event contingent upon
> it and observe any change in frequency. If there is a
> change, we classify the event as reinforcing to the
> organism under the existing conditions. There is noth-
> ing circular about classifying events in terms of their
> effects; the criterion is both empirical and objective. It
> would be circular, however, if we then went on to assert
> that a given event strengthens an operant *because* it is
> reinforcing.[25]

Reinforcers are of two kinds: positive and negative. Thus Skinner says

> some reinforcements consist of presenting stimuli, of
> adding something—for example, food, water, or sexual
> contact—to the situation. These we call *positive* rein-
> forcers. Others consist of *removing* something—for
> example, a loud noise, a very bright light, extreme cold

or heat, or electric shock—from the situation. These we call *negative* reinforcers. In both cases the effect of reinforcement is the same—the probability of response is increased.[26]

Further, according to Skinner:

> It is not correct to say that operant reinforcement "strengthens the response which precedes it." The response has already occurred and cannot be changed. What is changed is the future probability of responses in the same *class*. It is the operant as a class of behavior, rather than the response as a particular instance, which is conditioned. There is, therefore, no violation of the fundamental principle of science which rules out "final causes."[27]

According to Skinner, it is a mistake to equate positive reinforcement with pleasure or negative reinforcement with displeasure, for in either case an inference must be made which goes beyond the observed data and no new information is gained.[28]

Corresponding to the two types of reinforcement are two types of "punishment," both of which have the effect of decreasing the frequency of an operant which they follow. One form of punishment consists in presenting a specific aversive stimulus contingent upon the performance of a particular operant, thus decreasing its frequency. The other form of punishment consists of withdrawing something which is positively reinforcing to the organism, contingent upon the performance of a particular operant. According to Skinner, "the withdrawal of a positive reinforcer has by definition the same effect as the presentation of a negative."[29]

As in the case of reinforcement, punishment is determined in a functional or operational way for Skinner. If the environmental consequences of an operant decrease the probability of that operant occurring in the future, it is a punishment; if not, it is not a punishment. It may be noticed from this characterization of punishment that much of what is referred to as punishment in our society is actually not punishment in this strict sense, and is sometimes a form of reinforcement—as in the case of a child who seeks attention at any cost—even if the attention is a spanking.

In the case of most operant behavior, reinforcement or punishment does not occur following each case of a particular operant. Often we have to learn the specific conditions under which the behavior will be followed by the desired or undesired consequences. Such learning is referred to by Skinner as "operant discrimination." It takes place in what Skinner analyzes into a three term contingency. According to Skinner, "we describe the contingency by saying that a *stimulus* is the occasion upon which a *response* is followed by *reinforcement*...."[30]

We may learn, for example, that apples taste better when they are red than when they are green; or that we get a shock from the stove when our hands are wet but not when they are dry. Again, the similarity with Dewey's mediated impulses should be noted here. Skinner relates the process of operant discrimination to operant and respondent conditioning in the following way:

> The environment is so constructed that certain things tend to happen together. The organism is so constructed that its behavior changes when it comes into contact with such an environment. There are three principle cases. (1) Certain events—like the color and taste of ripe fruit—tend to occur together. Respondent conditioning is the corresponding effect upon behavior. (2) Certain activities of the organism effect certain changes in the environment. Operant conditioning is the corresponding effect upon behavior. (3) Certain events are the occasions upon which certain actions effect certain changes in the environment. Operant discrimination is the corresponding effect upon behavior. As a result of these processes, the organism which finds itself in a novel environment eventually comes to behave in an efficient way.[31]

The sign or signal which tells an organism that a certain activity will be reinforced or punished, in the process of operant discrimination, is referred to as a "discriminative stimulus." Frequently, a situation containing discriminative stimuli may become quite complex. Thus, for example, a reinforcement received as the result of performing a certain act in the presence of a discriminative stimulus may itself act as a discriminative stimulus for a further act. This latter act may then be reinforced with this reinforcement acting as a further discriminative stimulus. A succession of such reinforcers which act as discriminative stimuli is referred to by Skinner as a "chain." According to Skinner, "a response may produce or alter some of the variables which control another response. The result is a 'chain' one episode in our behavior generates conditions responsible for another."[32]

When behavior which has been maintained by reinforcement ceases to be reinforced, the result is said to be "extinction" of that operant. Extinction is different from forgetting, according to Skinner, since "in forgetting, the effect of conditioning is lost simply as time passes, whereas extinction requires that the response be emitted without reinforcement."[33]

Extinction of an operant occurs as a function of the type of schedule of reinforcement which had formerly maintained the behavior. Skinner has written extensively on the effects of different schedules of reinforcement on extinction in a work entitled *Schedules of Reinforcement*.[34] Although it is not necessary for the purposes of this discussion to present an extensive summary of the effects of the various schedules of reinforcement on extinction, it is worth noting a few basic factors.

An operant which has been maintained by being reinforced after each occurrence will tend to be extinguished quickly, when reinforcement is no longer forthcoming. Consider, for example, the behavior an individual emits when, after turning on a light switch, the light fails to go on. The behavior of turning on a light switch is usually reinforced by having the light go on. When the light fails to go on, the behavior of turning the switch quickly becomes extinguished.

More complex schedules of reinforcement involve situations where not every occurrence of an operant is reinforced. Rather, only certain occurrences are reinforced, as a function either of the time or of the activity of the individual. A schedule of reinforcement which involves reinforcement being presented as a function of time is referred to as an "interval schedule." If the interval of time between reinforcements is constant, the schedule is referred to as a "fixed interval schedule." If the interval is not fixed, but varies within a certain range of time, it is referred to as a "variable interval schedule." An example of a fixed interval schedule of reinforcement would be waiting for the morning paper to be delivered. Looking on the porch for the paper is reinforced after the passage of roughly twenty-four hours. "Still" fishing would be an example of a variable interval schedule. The time between catching individual fish varies, but one is reinforced as a function of the time spent waiting for a bite.

A schedule of reinforcement which involves reinforcement being presented as a function of the activity on the part of an individual is referred to as a "ratio schedule." There are both fixed and variable ratio schedules. One who receives a pay check at the end of a specific task, such as painting a house, is being reinforced on a fixed ratio schedule. If reinforcement is presented as a function of the performance of a specific task, but not after each performance, then a variable ratio schedule is being applied. Working a slot machine is an example of an operant which is reinforced on a variable ratio schedule.

Two additional points should be noted before leaving the topic of respondent and operant behavior. The first concerns the relationship between operant and respondent behavior on the one hand and voluntary and involuntary behavior on the other. The second concerns the relationship between operant and respondent behavior and the theory of evolution.

For Skinner, the distinction between voluntary behavior and involuntary behavior is legitimate so long as voluntary behavior is not thought of as "uncaused." Hence, Skinner says:

> In the present analysis we cannot distinguish between involuntary and voluntary behavior by raising the issue of who is in control. It does not matter whether behavior is due to a willing individual or a psychic usurper if we dismiss all inner agents of whatsoever sort. Nor can we make the distinction on the basis of control or lack of control, since we assume that no behavior is free. If we have no reason to distinguish between being able to do something and doing it, such expressions as "not being able to do something" or "not being able to help doing something" must be interpreted in some other way. When all relevant variables have been arranged, an organism will or will not respond. If it does not, it cannot. If it can, it will. To ask whether someone *can* turn a handspring is merely to ask whether there are circumstances under which he will do so.[35]

If the above provision is accepted, then it is possible to understand respondent behavior as equivalent to involuntary behavior and operant behavior as equivalent to voluntary behavior. On this point Skinner states that:

> The distinction between voluntary and involuntary behavior is a matter of the *kind* of control. It corresponds to the distinction between eliciting and discriminative stimuli. The eliciting stimulus appears to be more coercive. Its causal connection with behavior is relatively simple and easily observed. This may explain why it was discovered first. The discriminative stimulus, on the other hand, shares its control with other variables, so

that the inevitability of its effect cannot be easily demonstrated. But when all relevant variables have been taken into account, it is not difficult to guarantee the result—to force the discriminative operant as inexorably as the eliciting stimulus forces its response. If the manner in which this is done and the qualitative properties of the resulting relation warrant such a distinction, we may say that voluntary behavior is operant and involuntary behavior reflex.[36]

Skinner is also concerned with the purpose and nature of conditioning within the context of genetics and evolutionary theory. The behaving organism is not merely given, ready made, as it were; rather, "behavior requires a behaving organism which is the product of a genetic process."[37] The three processes involved in making the organism act more efficiently (operant conditioning, respondent conditioning, and operant discrimination) are themselves products of evolutionary development. Thus, Skinner points out that, "where inherited behavior leaves off, the inherited modifiability of the process of conditioning takes over."[38] These three processes (or the potentiality to respond to the environment in these three ways) have become part of our genetic heritage by furthering the survival of the species. As Skinner points out: "A behavioristic analysis rests on the following assumptions: A person is first of all an organism, a member of a species and a subspecies, possessing a genetic endowment of anatomical and physiological characteristics, which are the product of the contingencies of survival to which the species has been exposed in the process of evolution."[39]

Skinner draws an analogy between an organism's individual abilities to respond and adapt to its environment (through respondent or operant conditioning or operant discrimination) and the adaptation of a species and its subsequent survival through fortunate genetic mutations. The analogy focuses on the fact that for an organism to become conditioned it must first perform certain random actions, most of which are not reinforced. In a like manner, the members of a species may undergo specific mutations in the process of the transfer of genetic information. Most of these mutations are harmful or at least not beneficial to the survival of the species. When a genetic mutation renders the survival of an organism more secure, it also thereby promotes the survival of the species. Similarly, when an individual organism finally hits upon a form of behavior which is reinforcing, that behavior becomes more probable and the individual's chances for survival are promoted.

An individual organism may both be conditioned and be the result of genetic mutation. However, while it cannot pass on to its offspring the specific conditioning which it has received, it can pass on its genetic mutation. If the mutation is a beneficial one, such as the very susceptibility to respondent or operant conditioning or operant discrimination, then the future of the species is strongly favored. Accordingly, Skinner notes, "we may plausibly argue that a capacity to be reinforced by any feedback from the environment would be biologically advantageous, since it would prepare the organism to manipulate the environment successfully before a given state of deprivation developed."[40] Further, Skinner states that "the process of operant conditioning presumably evolved when those organisms which were more sensitively affected by the consequences of their behavior were better able to adjust to the environment and survive."[41]

Although the ability to learn from the environment has obvious advantages for the survival of the individual and the species, it also has at least a theoretical upper limit. That is, an organism which is hyper-responsive to its environment might learn behaviors not truly advantageous to its well being. "A quick response to reinforcement," as Skinner points out, "must have had survival value, and many species have reached the point at which a single reinforcement has a substantial effect. But the more rapidly an organism learns, the more vulnerable it is to adventitious contingencies."[42] This latter point reveals the evolutionary significance of various schedules of reinforcement. The fact that specific schedules of reinforcement produce lawful results tends to support the hypothesis that not merely the ability to respond to the environment, but the manner of an organism's response and its specific timing has also produced certain evolutionary advantages. An organism which responded only to continuous reinforcement, would not fare as well in a natural environment as an organism which could also respond to various intermittent schedules of reinforcement. At the other end of the continuum, an organism which maintained specific operants, although they had not been reinforced for extended periods of time, would also suffer ill effects in a natural setting.

2. Impulse, Instinct, and Reflex

Skinner does not use, as part of his explanatory terminology, the word 'impulse.' However, in what has been said above, it was noted that Skinner recognizes the existence of actions performed by organisms which correspond to what Dewey called 'impulses.' What Dewey called 'impulses' would for Skinner merely be activity which is emitted by the organism but has not yet led to a conditioning of the organism with respect to that activity. Thus he says for example, that

> an animal must emit a cry at least once for other reasons
> before the cry can be selected as a warning because of
> the advantage of the species. It follows that the entire
> repertoire of an individual or species must exist prior to
> ontogenic or phylogenic selection, but only in the form
> of minimal units.[43]

Under the heading of "innate" behavior, Skinner does, however, speak of instincts and reflexes. Of these he says "the principal difference between a reflex and an instinct is not in complexity of the response but in, respectively, the eliciting and releasing actions of the stimulus."[44] Thus, according to Skinner, while a reflex is elicited by the environment and is thus a part of respondent behavior, an instinct is released by the environment and is thus part of operant behavior.

Although Skinner recognizes that there may be legitimate uses for the terms 'reflex' and 'instinct,' he also notes that the abuse of these terms is widespread. This is the case primarily when the terms are affixed to various phenomena as if they were somehow explanations. That is, it is often thought by persons subscribing to some form of mentalistic psychology that to name an activity a 'reflex' or an 'instinct' is to cite an inner unseen agency which is responsible for the activity. An unfortunate consequence of this use of the two terms, moreover, is a tendency to mask the need for investigation into phenomena which are not understood. Thus Skinner points out:

> The newborn infant is so constructed that it takes in air
> and food and puts out wastes. Breathing, suckling,
> urination, and defecation are things the newborn infant
> *does,* but so, of course, are all its other physiological
> activities.
> When we know enough about the anatomy and physiol-
> ogy of the newborn, we shall be able to say *why* it breathes,
> suckles, urinates, and defecates, but at the moment we must
> be content with describing the behavior itself and investi-
> gating the conditions under which it occurs....[45]

If, however, we pronounce that a newborn performs its basic activities because of reflexes and instincts, and thereby blunt any desire to inquire further, we have misled ourselves.

Concerning instincts specifically, Skinner says:

> Behavior which is characteristic of a species is attributed to an instinct (of uncertain location or properties) said to be possessed by all members of the species. This is a flagrant example of explanatory fiction.... If the instinct of nest building refers only to the observed tendency of certain kinds of birds to build nests, it cannot explain why the birds build nests.[46]

A further problem with concentrating on explanations of behavior as examples of reflex activity is that it does not represent a sizable percentage of our overall behavior. Skinner notes that

> if we were to assemble all the behavior which falls into the pattern of the simple reflex, we should have only a very small fraction of the total behavior of the organism. This is not what early investigators in the field expected....The exhilarating discovery of the stimulus led to exaggerated claims. It is neither plausible nor expedient to conceive of the organism as a complicated jack-in-the-box with a long list of tricks, each of which may be evoked by pressing the proper button. The greater part of the behavior of the intact organism is not under the primitive sort of stimulus control.[47]

Further, Skinner points out that "when a large number of reflexes have once been identified and especially when it has been postulated that all behavior is reflex, the mere listing of reflexes has no further theoretical interest and remains important only for special investigations...."[48]

From these remarks it may be apparent why Skinner chooses to rely on his own terminology of 'respondent' and 'operant' behavior rather than attempting to affix merely descriptive or functional meanings to the terms 'instinct' and 'reflex' as well as other terms with long histories of association with mentalistic psychology or with early behaviorism.

3. Operant Behavior and Habit

According to Skinner, "the species acquires behavior (instincts) under contingencies of survival while the individual acquires behaviors (habits) under contingencies of reinforcement."[49] The term 'habit,' for

Skinner, is a legitimate term as long as it is understood as roughly equivalent to 'operant.' "An operant," for Skinner, "is a class, of which a response is an instance or 'member.'"[50] As a class of behaviors, an operant is an abstract notion. It represents one aspect of Skinner's "three term contingency" analysis of operant behavior. A given operant is the class of responses an instance of which is emitted under given environmental conditions and maintained by some form of reinforcement.

More specifically, to acquire an operant (or habit) as part of one's repertoire of behavior is not "merely to become accustomed to behaving in a given way."[51] Something must maintain the response class behavior under certain environmental conditions.

According to Skinner, an operant is shaped and maintained through being reinforced. In addition, "operant reinforcement not only strengthens a given response;" according to Skinner, but as noted above, "it brings the response under the control of a stimulus." However, he says that "the stimulus does not elicit the response as in a reflex; it merely sets the occasion upon which the response is more likely to occur."[52] The similarity with Dewey's concept of habit may be noticed here. For Dewey, a habit is not the mere repetition of an activity (see pp. 38–39 above). It involves rather a class of activities which are maintained by their effects and called out by specific circumstances.

Skinner amplifies his concept of an operant in the following statement where he relates the operant to the other two contingencies, occasion and consequences, which comprise his three term contingency analysis. Thus he says:

> The environment affects an organism after, as well as before, it responds. To stimulus and response we add consequences, and it is not just a third term in a sequence. The occasion upon which behavior occurs, the behavior itself, and its consequences are interrelated in the contingencies of reinforcement.... As the result of its place in these contingencies, a stimulus present when a response is reinforced acquires some control over the response. It does not then elicit the response as in a reflex; it simply makes it more probable that it will occur again, and it may do so in combination with other conditions affecting probability. A response reinforced upon a given occasion is most likely to occur on a very similar occasion, but because of a process called [stimulus] generalization it may appear on occasions sharing

only some of the same properties. If, however, it is reinforced only when a particular property is present, that property acquires exclusive control through a process called discrimination.[53]

The process involved in the acquisition of a given operant described above can be seen to resemble, in a general way, the process involved when one acquires a habit on Dewey's analysis. The latter, it will be recalled, involves a process of impulse mediation. For Dewey, impulses are mediated and an organism's behavior comes gradually to be under the influence of its past interactions with the environment. Regularities in the environment lead to regularities in behavior, or habits.

Although Skinner's concept of an operant is generally compatible with Dewey's concept of a habit, Skinner finds certain other uses of the term 'habit' objectionable. He objects, for example, to uses of 'habit' which seem to imply that a habit is an internal force or stored predisposition to action. These illicit uses of the term share the common feature of confusing the use of the term 'habit' when intended merely to express an observed regularity of behavior with the term's use as an attempted explanation of that same regularity. Skinner cites two examples of this kind of misuse of the concept of habit in the following discussions:

> The statement that the bird "learns that it will get food by stretching its neck" is an inaccurate report of what has happened. To say that it has acquired the "habit" of stretching its neck is merely to resort to an explanatory fiction, since our only evidence of the habit is the acquired tendency to perform the act.[54]

And again:

> The cigarette habit is presumably something more than the behavior said to show that a person possesses it; but the only other information we have concerns the reinforcers and schedules of reinforcement which make a person smoke a great deal. The contingencies are not stored; they have simply left a changed person.[55]

A further point which Skinner makes concerning habits, operants, or classes of behavior, is that they need not consist of behaviors of identical physical topography, but rather may have only a functional similarity. Thus an individual's habits of shaving in the morning may sometimes involve the use of shaving lather and a razor blade and other times the use of an electric razor. The two processes are quite different, but compose the same habit or operant and result in the same finished product. This phenomenon is accounted for by Skinner with the notion of response generalization. According to Skinner,

> reinforcement strengthens responses which differ in topography from the responses reinforced. When we reinforce pressing a lever, for example, or saying *Hello,* responses differing quite widely in topography grow more probable. This is a characteristic of behavior which has strong survival value since it would be very hard for an organism to acquire an effective repertoire if reinforcement strengthened only identical responses.[56]

4. *Emotion, Desire, Purpose, and Motive*

The terms 'emotion,' desire,' 'purpose,' and 'motive' all share the common property of being popularly taken as names for explanatory agencies within the individual. They are all used, at various times, that is, in answer to questions asking why an individual may have performed some particular act. As with other psychological terms which Skinner analyzes, he finds that this misuse of the above terms stems from certain mentalistic assumptions.

In the case of emotions, for example, people are often asserted to be behaving in certain ways because of a particular emotion, for example, frustration. Frustration is thus thought of as a mental cause of the behavior. On Skinner's analysis the frustration which an individual feels and the behavior he/she performs are joint effects of the same cause—a condition in the environment. Furthermore, he points out that "frustration is a single process in the whole organism," rather than a mental state and its physical outcome.[57]

Concerning emotions generally, Skinner points out that they "are excellent examples of the fictional causes to which we commonly attribute behavior."[58] The problem with concentrating an analysis of behavior on "emotional causes," for Skinner, is not that people don't really experience emotions, but that this is not the right place to look for a solution to the problem of explaining behavior. Thus, he points out:

As long as we conceive of the problem of emotion as one of inner states, we are not likely to advance a practical technology. It does not help in the solution of a practical problem to be told that some feature of a man's behavior is due to frustration or anxiety; we also need to be told how the frustration or anxiety has been induced and how it may be altered. In the end, we find ourselves dealing with two events—the emotional behavior and the manipulable conditions of which that behavior is a function—which comprise the proper subject matter of the study of emotion.[59]

Rather than dealing with emotions as mental states, the correct method for understanding emotions is to place them in a functional or operational context. On this score Skinner gives William James credit for beginning the process of correctly pointing out the relation of emotions to behavior.[60] The correct account, according to Skinner, is that "emotion is a matter of the probability of engaging in certain kinds of behavior defined by certain kinds of consequences. Anger is a heightened probability of attack, fear is a heightened probability of running away, and love is a heightened probability of positively reinforcing a loved person."[61]

Skinner explains the concept of desire in a similar way. It is not an explanation of behavior to say that someone performed a given act because of a desire—since the desire is inferred as a result of the activity. At best, the term 'desire' may be used, according to Skinner, to report the unusual strength of a behavior.[62] A desire is thus not properly an inner state but rather the observed intensity with which a particular behavior is carried out.

According to Skinner, "possibly no charge is more often leveled against behaviorism than that it cannot deal with purpose or intention."[63] However, as he points out, while "a stimulus-response formula has no answer operant behavior is the very field of purpose and intention."[64] This is so in the sense that operant behavior is that behavior which is controlled by its outcome. "Purpose," however, as Skinner points out, "is not a property of the behavior itself; it is a way of referring to controlling variables."[65] These controlling variables are the reinforcers which have followed certain forms of behavior in the past. Thus, Skinner says, "the purpose of skilled movement of the hand is to be found in the consequences which follow it."[66] As an example of this, he says

a pianist neither acquires nor executes the behavior of playing a scale smoothly because of a prior intention of

116

doing so. Smoothly played scales are reinforcing for
many reasons, and they select skilled movements.... He
does not play a smooth scale because he feels the
purpose of doing so; what he feels is a by-product of his
behavior in relation to its consequences.[67]

Skinner's point here may be put another way. Purpose is not properly
understood as being directed toward the activities which produce reinforcing consequences (like piano playing) but rather toward the reinforcing
consequences themselves. Or, as Skinner points out, "when a person is
'aware of his purpose' he is feeling or observing introspectively a condition produced by reinforcement."[68]

Thus, in general, Skinner's position would appear to be that the
behavior which is properly called "purposive" differs from that called
"random," because the former is behavior which is under the control of the
organism's past history of reinforcement. For example, he points out that

we learn to look for an object when we acquire behavior
which commonly has the consequences discovering it.
Thus, to look for a match is to look in a manner
previously reinforced by finding matches.... If past
consequences have not been very explicit, we are likely
to look in vague and unproductive ways.[69]

Skinner's treatment of motives shares certain properties with Dewey's.
Like Dewey, Skinner recognizes the mistake of trying to define what are
called motives as being either purely internal states of an individual, or
purely external objects or states. Money, for example, while it is often said
to motivate people, by itself has no particular effect on behavior. To serve
as a motivation it must first be used in ways which allow it to become a
generalized reinforcer, and this can only be done by using it in connection
with goods or activities which are primarily reinforcing to a given
individual. This relation between the internal and external aspects of
motivation is expressed by Skinner when he says that "motives are in
people while contingencies of reinforcement are in the environment, but
motives are at best the effects of reinforcement."[70]

5. Self, Self Knowledge, Consciousness, and Mind
The self, according to Skinner, has long stood as a concept designed
to cover our ignorance of the nature of the forces which control our

behavior. Thus, he says: "If we cannot show what is responsible for a man's behavior, we say that he himself is responsible for it. The precursors of physical science once followed the same practice, but the wind is no longer blown by Aeolus, nor is the rain cast down by Jupiter Pluvius."[71]

As already mentioned, Skinner believes that the controlling forces are to be found in the environment in which a person lives. Because of this what is called the self is not an autonomous agent directing our lives, but rather a set of responses we have learned through interaction with our environment. Specifically, he says "self is simply a device for representing a *functionally unified system of responses*."[72] Or again he says "a self is a repertoire of behavior appropriate to a given set of contingencies. "[73]

However, the situation is not as simple as it may at first appear. "The identity conferred upon a self," according to Skinner; "arises from the contingencies responsible for the behavior."[74] But what of situations where the self shows a lack of unity, as when we are "angry with ourself," or "not ourself today," or torn between two repertoires of behavior which we have learned under different circumstances? Accordingly, Skinner says:

> Whatever the self may be, it is apparently not identical with the physical organism. The organism behaves, while the self initiates or directs behavior. Moreover, more than one self is needed to explain the behavior of one organism. A mere inconsistency in conduct from one moment to the next is perhaps no problem, for a single self could dictate different kinds of behavior from time to time. But there appear to be two selves acting simultaneously and in different ways when one self controls another or is aware of the activity of another.[75]

And further:

> Organized systems of responses may be related to each other in the same way as are single responses and for the same reasons.... For example, two response systems may be incompatible. If the relevant variables are never present at the same time, the incompatibility is unimportant. If the environment of which behavior is a function is not consistent from moment to moment, there is no reason to expect consistency in behavior. The

pious churchgoer on Sunday may become an aggressive, unscrupulous businessman on Monday. He possesses two response systems appropriate to different sets of circumstances, and his inconsistency is not greater than that of the environment which takes him to church on Sunday and to work on Monday. But the controlling variables may come together; during a sermon, the churchgoer may be asked to examine his business practices, or the businessman may engage in commercial transactions with his clergyman or his church.[76]

This latter example, it may be noticed, is not merely a question of conflicting selves; it falls within the purview of Dewey's concept of a moral problem. Thus, the individual in Skinner's example (to use Dewey's mode of characterizing the problem) is attracted to two opposing goods: his business and his church. But while Dewey suggests general methods for the resolution of such problems, Skinner, except for suggesting an overall transformation of the culture *a la Walden Two,* does not.[77]

Given the above characterization of one's self (or more accurately, one's selves) it is appropriate to ask what effect our consciousness of self has on our behavior? It appears to be the case for Skinner that self consciousness is not an integral part of being human, but is rather something we learn (perhaps even reluctantly) through our interactions with our social environment. In particular the nature of our consciousness appears to be a function of the type of verbal community found in our social environment. Accordingly, Skinner notes that "it requires a special verbal environment to impose consciousness on behavior by inducing a person to respond to his own body while he is behaving. If consciousness seems to have a causal effect, it is the effect of the special environment which induces self-observation"[78] Further, according to Skinner:

> Self-knowledge is of social origin. It is only when a person's private world becomes important to others that it is made important to him. It then enters into the control of behavior called knowing. But self-knowledge has a special value to the individual himself. A person who has been "made aware of himself" by the questions he has been asked is in a better position to predict and control his own behavior.[79]

The result of this conception of consciousness, for Skinner, is that "without the help of a verbal community all behavior would be unconscious.... It is not only not the special field of autonomous man, it is not within the range of solitary man."[80]

Further, as Skinner points out, our knowledge of the nature and sources of self-knowledge enables us to clarify what exactly it is we are knowing in our self-knowledge. This in turn has some important consequences. Skinner says for example:

> Our increasing knowledge of the control exerted by the environment makes it possible to examine the effect of the world within the skin and the nature of self-knowledge. It also makes it possible to interpret a wide range of mentalistic expressions. For example, we can look at those features of behavior which have led people to speak of an act of will, of a sense of purpose, of experience as distinct from reality, of innate or acquired ideas, of memories, meanings, and the personal knowledge of the scientist, and hundreds of other mentalistic things or events. Some can be "translated into behavior," others can be discarded as unnecessary or meaningless.[81]

From the statements above it can be seen that Skinner is not (as perhaps some early behaviorists were) attempting to write off our consciousness. "Rather than ignore consciousness," Skinner says, "an experimental analysis of behavior has stressed certain crucial issues. The question is not whether a man can know himself but what he knows when he does so."[82]

From this discussion of consciousness it is now possible to understand why Skinner feels it is unnecessary to attribute the sources of our behavior to an internal agency—the mind. Not only do mentalistic accounts of behavior fail to make prediction and control of that behavior possible, they also stand in the way of investigations which would promote these ends. Hence, says Skinner: "By attempting to move human behavior into a world of nonphysical dimensions, mentalistic or cognitive psychologists have cast the basic issues in insoluble forms."[83] In addition, however, he points out:

> The exploration of the emotional and motivational life of the mind has been described as one of the great achievements in the history of human thought but it is

possible that it has been one of the great disasters. In its search for internal explanation, supported by the false sense of cause associated with feelings and introspective observations, mentalism has obscured the environmental antecedents which would have led to a much more effective analysis. The objection to the inner workings of the mind is not that they are not open to inspection but that they have stood in the way of the inspection of more important things.[84]

In part, what makes the use of mental explanations seem so fruitless to Skinner is the fact that they are often based on inferences from observable behavior. Thus, mentalistic psychologists have observed physical behavior and made inferences about an unobserved inner construct, the mind. Subsequently, they have turned these inferences back upon the original observed behavior and attempted to explain it with mental agencies. On this point Skinner says that "mental life and the world in which it is lived are inventions. They have been invented on the analogy of external behavior occurring under external contingencies."[85]

The above process is seen to be more useless when it recognized that "thinking is behaving," for Skinner, and "the mistake is in allocating the behavior to the mind."[86] Rather than interpreting thinking as a mental process, Skinner prefers to understand it as covert behavior. He says that

the term ['thinking' usually] refers to completed behavior which occurs on a scale so small that it cannot be detected by others. Such behavior is called covert.... Covert behavior has the advantage that we can act without committing ourselves; we can revoke the behavior and try it again if private consequences are not reinforcing.... Covert behavior is almost always acquired in overt form.... Covert behavior is also easily observed and by no means unimportant, and it was a mistake for methodological behaviorism and certain versions of logical positivism and structuralism to neglect it simply because it was not "objective."[87]

6. *Control, Self Control, and Moral Control*

Skinner notes that "we cannot choose a way of life in which there is no control. We can only change the controlling conditions."[88] Skinner's position regarding the mind and consciousness, as outlined above, raises a question about the nature of control. If the mind is not an agency of internal control and if even consciousness itself is not necessary for behavior, wherein lies the control of behavior? Skinner's answer, as previously suggested, is that ultimately control lies in the environment. Thus he says: "A scientific analysis of behavior must, I believe, assume that a person's behavior is controlled by his genetic and environmental histories rather than by the person himself as an initiating, creative agent...."[89]

The environment, however, can be used to effect control in more than one way, as mentioned above; the frequently used means of control are not necessarily the best means. Accordingly Skinner points out that:

> Organized agencies or institutions, such as govern-
> ments, religions, and economic systems, and to a
> lesser extent educators and psychotherapists, exert a
> powerful and often troublesome control. It is exerted
> in ways which most effectively reinforce those who
> exert it, and unfortunately this usually means in ways
> which either are immediately aversive to those con-
> trolled or exploit them in the long run.
> Those who are so controlled then take action. They
> escape from the controller—moving out of range if
> he is an individual, or defecting from a govern-
> ment, becoming an apostate from a religion, re-
> signing, or playing truant—or they may attack in
> order to weaken or destroy the controlling power,
> as in a revolution, a reformation, a strike, or a
> student protest. In other words, they oppose con-
> trol with counter-control.[90]

Skinner's answer to this problem lies in the increased use of positive reinforcement as a means of control, since it does not have the drawbacks of aversive control mentioned above. An important point to notice about Skinner's view of control is that whether it is done negatively or positively, it is not done by trying to deal directly with a person's mind. "One person manages another in the sense in which he manages himself," according to Skinner. "He does not do so by changing feelings or states of mind.... One person changes the behavior of another by changing the world in which he lives. In doing so, he no doubt changes what the other person feels or introspectively observes."[91]

A significant point which emerges from the above statement concerns what people do when they control themselves. Accordingly; Skinner says:

> When a man controls himself, chooses a course of action, thinks out the solution to a problem, or strives toward an increase in self-knowledge, he is *behaving*. He controls himself precisely as he would control the behavior of anyone else—through the manipulation of variables of which behavior is a function. His behavior in so doing is a proper object of analysis, and eventually must be accounted for with variables lying outside the individual himself.[92]

However, as noted in the discussion of the self, above, one individual is not necessarily one self. For Skinner, "when we say that a man controls himself, we must specify who is controlling whom."[93] If it is a case of one self having control over another self, it is still important for Skinner that these selves are traceable to the environmental history of the individual. Thus, for Skinner

> the managed self is composed of what is significantly called selfish behavior—the product of the biological reinforcers to which the species has been made sensitive through natural selection. The managing self, on the other hand, is set up mainly by the social environment, which has *its* selfish reasons for teaching a person to alter his behavior in such a way that it becomes less aversive and possibly more reinforcing to others.[94]

The managing self, since it is the organized system of responses we learn through our interactions with the social environment, is the locus of what may be called our ethical behavior. For Skinner our ethical behavior (and thus our ethical thinking) is ultimately the result of the social environment in which we developed and live. Accordingly, mentalistically oriented moral thinkers who have attributed our ethical behavior to mental causes such as a sense of duty, moral intuitions, a sense of sin, a conscience, or a moral sense, have unwittingly been dealing with the effects rather than the causes of moral behavior. While it is true that we may introspectively be aware of the above feelings, Skinner's analysis shows that they are merely the results of our interactions with our social environment. As a consequence, moralists who accept some form of mentalistic psychology have been all but helpless in trying to make people more moral, since their approaches deal, usually, with people's minds not with their environments. "One of the most tragic consequences of mentalism," according to Skinner, "is dramatically illustrated by those who are earnestly concerned about the plight of the world today and who see no help except in a return to morality, ethics, or a sense of decency, as personal possessions." What is needed instead "is a restoration of social environments in which people behave in ways called moral."[95]

It may be recalled from Chapter Three that according to Dewey all our behavior is potentially moral. But obviously most people do not see their behavior in this way. If Dewey was suggesting, as he no doubt was, that it would be desirable if more people did view all of their acts as having potentially moral significance, Skinner suggests the proper way to accomplish this end. As Skinner notes: "Different people show different amounts and kinds of moral and ethical behavior, depending upon the extent of their exposure to such contingencies."[96] The instrument needed to bring people to a fuller awareness of the potential moral nature of all behavior is thus the manipulation of factors in the social environment. Put another way, Skinner suggests that we shift the whole emphasis of our thinking about morals from the individual seen as a responsible agent, to the environment. Accordingly, he says: "And if we are asked: 'Is a person moral because he behaves morally, or does he behave morally because he is moral?' we must answer, 'Neither,' He behaves morally and we call him moral because he lives in a particular kind of environment."[97] If it is asked how the social environment is able to exercise this kind of control, Skinner's answer is that "the group exercises an ethical control over each of its members mainly through its power to reinforce or punish. The power is derived from sheer number and from the importance of other people in the life of each member."[98] However, this power has not always been used effectively. As a result Skinner says "ethical control by the group has moved only very slowly from coercive techniques, in which the individual is forced to behave in conformity with the interests of others, to techniques in which 'good' is more important than 'bad.'"[99]

In the foregoing discussion it has been assumed that it was clear what Skinner means by 'ethical behavior.' This is an assumption Skinner himself makes, as he does not present an explicit definition of the term. However, it is important for what follows to make as explicit as possible what Skinner does mean or at least seems to mean by the term 'ethical behavior.' First, it should be noted that he is not speaking of behavior which he personally sees as good or worthwhile. This is not to say, however, that he sees what he is calling ethical behavior as somehow undesirable either. He seems, so far as is possible, to be using the term in a way which is neutral with respect to his own personal values. Second, the behavior which he speaks of as ethical behavior is that which involves the interaction of people within a social environment. A solitary individual growing up on his/her own would not exhibit ethical behavior. Third, the behavior he refers to as "ethical" behavior is that which shows outward signs of "taking account" of the behavior of others. It can be contrasted with the "selfish" behavior of an infant, who has not yet learned to adjust his/her actions to the actions of others. Ethical behavior, that is, is a certain kind of behavior which has been molded by a social environment. On this Skinner says "man has not evolved as an ethical or moral animal. He has evolved to the point at which he has constructed an ethical or moral culture."[100]

More specifically, the behavior called "ethical" (which is molded by a social environment) is at least in part under the control of conditioning which involved the terms 'good,' 'bad,' 'right,' and 'wrong,' or their equivalents. Skinner expresses and expands this last point in this way:

> The principal technique employed in the control of the individual by any group of people who have lived together for a sufficient length of time is as follows. The behavior of the individual is classified as either "good" or "bad" or, to the same effect, "right" or "wrong" and is reinforced or punished accordingly. We need not seek far for a definition of these controversial terms. The behavior of an individual is usually called good or right insofar as it reinforces other members of the group and bad or wrong insofar as it is aversive. The actual practices of the group may not be completely consistent with these definitions. The initial classification may have been accidental: a conspicuous bit of behavior which was only adventitiously correlated with reinforcing or aversive events came to be classed as good or bad accordingly. Our definition applies literally to the origin of such a superstitious practice but does not fit any current effect. A classification of behavior may also continue in force long after it is out of date: behavior often continues to be branded good or bad although, through some change in conditions, it is no longer reinforcing or aversive.[101]

Two significant points emerge from these statements. One involves the assumption of a naturalistic account of moral language. On this account moral terms like 'good' are linked to the reinforcing aspects of people's actions, while moral terms like 'bad' are used in response to the aversive aspects of people's actions. On this analysis of moral language Skinner says:

> We say that there is something "morally wrong" about
> a totalitarian state, a gambling enterprise, uncontrolled
> piecework wages, the sale of harmful drugs, or undue
> personal influence, not because any absolute set of
> values, but because all these things have aversive con-
> sequences.[102]

The other point made is that for Skinner, just as it is natural for people to attempt to exert control on one another, it is also reinforcing when this control succeeds.[103]

In addition, if it is possible for someone to exert this control simply by the use of verbal behavior, as in saying "good" or "bad" in response to the actions of others, the efficiency of this mode of control will itself be further reinforcing to the controller. Skinner confirms this speculation when he says:

> Perhaps the commonest generalized reinforcers are
> verbal stimuli "Good," "Right," "Bad," and "Wrong."
> These are used, together with unconditioned and other
> conditioned reinforcers such as praise, thanks, caresses,
> gratitudes, favors, blows, blame, censure, and criticism,
> to shape the behavior of the individual.[104]

At this point, however, Skinner has apparently committed himself as far as he intends on matters of ethics. He has recognized a connection between what is reinforcing or aversive and what is called "good" or "bad" respectively. In addition, he has recognized the powerful effects of moral language when used as generalized reinforcers or punishers. Further, Skinner has accepted the idea that once a moral value system has been stipulated, whether by a religion or government or some other source, behavioristic practices can be used to condition effective acceptance of that system. Skinner stops short of claiming that a purely behavioristic analysis can provide specific moral values in any traditional sense. Concerning the traditional concerns of ethics and the relation of behaviorism to them, Skinner says:

What do we mean by Good? How may we encourage people to practice the Good Life? Our account does not answer questions of this sort in the spirit in which they are usually asked. Within the framework of a natural science certain kinds of behavior are observed when people live together in groups—kinds of behavior which are directed toward the control of the individual and which operate for the advantage of other members of the group. We define "good" and "bad," or "right" and "wrong," with respect to a particular set of practices. We account for the practices by noting the effects which they have upon the individual and in turn upon the members of the group according to the basic processes of behavior.[105]

Or again:

Ethics is usually concerned with justifying controlling practices rather than with merely describing them. Why is a particular bit of behavior classed as good or bad? The question is sometimes answered by asserting that "good" and "bad" have been defined by supernatural authorities. Although a science of behavior might help in designing educational practices which would encourage people to be good and dissuade them from being bad according to a given authority, it can scarcely pass upon the validity of such a definition.[106]

When the various elements of Skinner's position concerning ethics as it relates to psychology are pieced together, the following picture emerges. Both ethics and psychology are concerned with the control of human behavior, though from different perspectives. All behavior is under the control of the organism's environment or the environmental history of the organism. Neither ethics nor psychology when dealing with the control of a human individual is dealing with an autonomous agent whose behavior is directed by a self-sufficient mind which is responsible for its choices. The results of a behavioristic analysis of behavior place in our possession the means by which the most effective control can be gained over individual members of a group. This control is effective for the reason that it does not give rise to attempts at counter control, or revolt, or social friction in general. As a consequence of this form of control, based primarily on the use of positive reinforcers, individuals are optimally happy; the most effective road to the production of happiness has been one of the long standing problems of ethical theory. While Skinner does not believe the use of positive reinforcement is a panacea, and while he realizes that its use in effecting control can lead to difficulties,[107] he nonetheless recognizes it as the most effective mode of control, from both a moral and psychological point of view.

Skinner's utopian novel *Walden Two* depicts a small society of persons living under the principles of his proposed technology of behavior.[108] Skinner himself believes that the proper approach toward reorganizing our culture in line with his behavioristic principles of control will include creating small communities operating in much the same way as the community described in *Walden Two*.[109] In addition, Skinner believes that by "'nibbling' at cultural practices in general—as in education, therapy and so on," we may also advance the cause of his cultural ideal.[110]

At this point it may be wondered whether Skinner has not committed himself to a set of values and at the same time denied that a natural science of behavior can support such values. Skinner would likely deny that this is what he has done. He claims only to be describing the consequences of various forms of organism-environment interaction.[111] When it is asked, for example, who is to set up the environment which will make control planned rather than accidental, Skinner's reply is that scientists should not be ruled out as controllers and planners simply because they are scientists. He points out, concerning the instituting of planned control for example, that,

> as the emphasis shifts to the environment, the individual seems to be exposed to a new kind of danger. Who is to construct the controlling environment and to what end? Autonomous man presumably controls himself in accordance with a built-in set of values; he works for what he finds good. But what will the putative controller find good, and will it be good for those he controls? Answers to questions of this sort are said, of course, to call for value judgments.[112]

Four significant points should be noticed in regard to the above statement.

First, as will be more fully developed in Chapter Five, value judgments, according to Skinner, are merely "statement[s] made because of reinforcing consequences which arise either from genetic endowment or cultural contingencies."[113] That is, to call something a value judgment is not to suppose any particular wisdom on the part of its utterer. Value judgments we express, like all behavior we emit, are to be understood in terms of our personal history of interaction with the environment. Presumably the value judgments we pronounce have no more or less significance than our other conditioned behaviors.

Second, Skinner's answer to questions about who will control the controllers in a controlled environment, and who in turn will control them, is that they are not such important or profound questions as they may first seem. This is the case for two reasons.

The first is that it is possible, as in the fictional community described in *Walden Two*, to arrange the contingencies which control behavior so that they also control the behavior of the controllers. In *Walden Two* the designer of the community, Frazier, was put in a position similar to that of God in Deistic religious conceptions. His role was to design a community, and bring it into being. Once the community was in operation he no longer played a part, except as one more member of the community.

The second point concerns the nature of the control being suggested. The very control which Skinner is stressing as most effective is, by a happy coincidence, that which avoids punishment, and subsequently eliminates the evils associated with the means by which people attempt to avoid punishing contingencies: escape and avoidance. The mere fact that our institutions would not require the use of threats and punishments to "induce" cooperation (as our school systems use the threat of bad grades to "motivate" students) would seem to recommend Skinner's proposed technology of behavior, at least *prima facie*.

In commenting on the role of psychology in ethics, Skinner makes two important claims. First, he denies that the use of "a more effective technology [of behavior] will eliminate the need to ask questions concerning moral responsibility though," he states, "the questions will be phrased differently."[114] The second claim which Skinner makes is that "our task is not to encourage moral struggle or to build or demonstrate inner virtues. It is to make life less punishing and in doing so to release for more reinforcing activities the time and energy consumed in the avoidance of punishment."[115]

In saying that, it is our task to make life less punishing, it is worth asking whether Skinner is now speaking as a scientist or as a moralist or whether it is truly possible to divide the two? The answer to this question, so far as it relates to the general "is-ought" controversy, will be dealt with more fully in the next chapter.

7. *Freedom, Responsibility, and the Will*

If it is asked, in reference to the discussion above, "Is the happiness to be obtained through a behavioristically designed social system worth the price?" we are led directly into a consideration of the possible alternatives. What price exactly are we talking about? On the surface it may appear that the price is our freedom—in some sense. After all, it may be thought, we are trading our right to choose and be free (and perhaps unhappy) for a controlled environment where we are satisfied with our lot in life, free from punishment and aversive controlling techniques. This way of putting the situation, however, misrepresents the case. Skinner begins with the claim that all environments are controlled—in the sense that an organism's behavior can be accounted for on the basis of its previous interactions with the environment.[116] This means that if there is a question of freedom to be raised, it is not the case that what freedom we have is lessened as we move from a social environment which is basically inefficient and uses aversive techniques of control, to one which is efficient and uses positive reinforcement as a means of control. The control is present in either case, it is simply the observable nature of the case that the former type of control leads to resistance on the part of those controlled, which is not the case in the latter form of control.[117] On this point Skinner says

> the fundamental mistake made by all those who choose
> weak methods of control is to assume that the balance of
> control is left to the individual, when in fact it is left to
> other conditions. The other conditions are often hard to
> see, but to continue to neglect them and to attribute their
> effects to autonomous man is to court disaster.[118]

The conclusion to be drawn from this position seems to be that since control is present in every social environment, the degree of freedom (the so-called "metaphysical freedom of will") will remain constant regardless of whether the means of control applied by the environment are primarily aversive or not. The fact that a person resists aversive control is not any more an indication of freedom than the fact that the same individual does not resist control through positive reinforcement. Both are equally lawful phenomena. What has apparently led some moral theorists astray is an over reliance on the presence or absence of feelings of freedom—a reliance on introspective evidence. In explanation of this point Skinner says:

> Man's struggle for freedom is not due to a will to be free,
> but to certain behavioral processes characteristic of the

human organism, the chief effect of which is the avoidance of or escape from so-called "aversive" features of the environment. Physical and biological technologies have been mainly concerned with natural aversive stimuli; the struggle for freedom is concerned with stimuli intentionally arranged by other people.... It has been successful in reducing the aversive stimuli used in intentional control, but it has made the mistake of defining freedom in terms of states of mind or feelings, and it has therefore not been able to deal effectively with techniques of control which do not breed escape or revolt but nevertheless have aversive consequences. It has been forced to brand all control as wrong and to misrepresent many of the advantages to be gained from social environment.[119]

Further, he points out:

It is possible that man's genetic endowment supports this kind of struggle for freedom: when treated aversively people tend to act aggressively or to be reinforced by signs of having worked aggressive damage. Both tendencies should have had evolutionary advantages, and they can easily be demonstrated.[120]

It can be seen from these comments why Skinner believes that the feeling of freedom is not a true indicator of the extent of one's freedom. It may well be, as Skinner seems to be suggesting, that the feeling of freedom is tied up with the reinforcing aspects of escape from aversive control. But to escape from aversive control is not to escape from control. "The feeling of freedom becomes an unreliable guide to actions," according to Skinner, "as soon as would-be controllers turn to nonaversive measures, as they are likely to do to avoid the problems raised when the controllee escapes or attacks."[121] Thus it would appear that in Skinner's ideal social environment (where control is effected through positive reinforcement), the feeling of freedom might well be missing. However, if we substitute "feeling accompanying the escape from aversive control" for the "feeling of freedom," it becomes obvious that the issue of freedom (apart from the feeling of freedom) itself is unaffected.

Aside from the "feeling of freedom," another aspect of the situation which has clouded the issue of freedom is the fact that the less obvious the control is in a particular situation, the more likely we are (given our common mentalistic ways of thinking) to attribute the control to the individual himself/herself. Thus Skinner says "we recognize a person's dignity or worth when we give him credit for what he has done. The amount we give is inversely proportional to the conspicuousness of the causes of his behavior. If we do not know why a person acts as he does, we attribute his behavior to him."[122] The belief in self-caused behavior is a belief in what Skinner calls the "autonomous man." "We stand in awe of the inexplicable," according to Skinner, "and it is therefore not surprising that we are likely to admire behavior more as we understand it less. And, of course, what we do not understand we attribute to autonomous man."[123] Since the behavior in which the question of freedom arises is our voluntary behavior, or in Skinner's terminology our "operant behavior," there are many times when the causes are less than obvious. In the extreme of this situation, Skinner notes that "we give maximal credit when there are quite visible reasons for behaving differently."[124] This phenomenon can be explained if we consider once again the nature of operant behavior. Hence Skinner says:

> The illusion that freedom and dignity are respected when control seems incomplete arises in part from the probabilistic nature of operant behavior. Seldom does any environmental condition "elicit" behavior in the all-or-nothing fashion of a reflex; it simply makes a bit of behavior more likely to occur. A hint will not itself suffice to evoke a response, but it adds strength to a weak response which may then appear.[125]

One unfortunate consequence of the traditional mentalistic conception of autonomous man, for Skinner, is the fact that, attending the freedom which he/she is accorded when his/her actions have unobserved causes, is the ascription of personal responsibility. With this responsibility comes the justification of punishment—and a continuance of the use of aversive control. In reference to this problem Skinner has the following to say: "In the traditional view, a person is free. He is autonomous in the sense that his behavior is uncaused. He can therefore be held responsible for what he does and justly punished if he offends."[126] This view is unfortunate, for Skinner, because it attempts to place responsibility for actions on individual persons. He says accordingly: "Those who undertake to do something about human behavior—for any reason whatsoever—become part of the environment to which responsibility shifts.... The mistake... is to put the responsibility anywhere, to suppose that somewhere a causal sequence is initiated."[127]

Skinner is not optimistic that this way of dealing with individuals will soon be rectified. The ways of thinking associated with autonomous man are quite firmly established in the social environment. Thus according to Skinner,

> we have moved forward by dispossessing autono-
> mous man, but he has not departed gracefully. He is
> conducting a sort of rear-guard action in which un-
> fortunately, he can marshal formidable support. He is
> still an important figure in political science, law,
> religion, economics, anthropology, sociology, psy-
> chotherapy, philosophy, ethics, history, education,
> child care, linguistics, architecture, city planning,
> and family life.[128]

In all of the above areas the concepts of freedom and responsibility are still quite important. In each of them the issue of free will is still alive.

In the end Skinner's position on freedom of the will is quite close to Dewey's. The problem for both men is not so much whether there truly is a metaphysical freedom or not, but, whether believing that there is or is not actually makes a difference—does it explain anything that could not be explained in some other fashion? For Dewey a belief in this kind of freedom is simply not helpful; for Skinner it is positively harmful. Belief in free will cuts off further investigation into the causes of behavior. Further, it leads, as noted above, to the ascription of individual responsibility and in turn to the administering of punishment. In summarizing these points Skinner says:

> By attributing otherwise unexplained behavior to an
> act of will or choice, one seems to resolve puzzle-
> ment. That is perhaps the *raison d'être* of the con-
> cept; behavior is satisfactorily accounted for as long
> as we have no reason to explain the act of will. But the
> conditions which determine the form of probability
> of an operant are in a person's history. Since they are
> not conspicuously represented in the current setting,
> they are easily overlooked. It is then easy to believe
> that the will is free and that the person is free to
> choose.[129]

8. Decision Making, Problem Solving, and Moral Problems

Given Skinner's account of freedom and his emphasis on the controlling nature of the environment, it may be wondered what occurs when an individual makes a decision or solves a problem. If such a process is not to be explained by the agency of a free will, how then is it to be accounted for? Skinner's answer is compatible with what he said about control: that we solve problems and make decisions by altering aspects of the environment, which in turn alter our responses. Thus, he says:

> A person has a problem when some condition will be reinforcing but he lacks a response that will produce it. He will solve the problem when he emits such a response.... Solving a problem is, however, more than *emitting* the response which is the solution; it is a matter of taking steps to make that response more probable, usually by changing the environment.[130]

And further:

> It is said that a person has made a choice when he has taken one of two or more seemingly possible courses of action. The trouble lies in the word possible. Simply to make one of several "possible" responses—as in walking aimlessly through a park—requires no serious act of decision, but when consequences are important and the probabilities of two or more responses are nearly equal, a problem must be solved. A person usually solves it and escapes from indecision by changing the setting.[131]

The ideal of escaping from indecision is quite important, according to Skinner's account. As in Dewey's concept of the quest for certainty, Skinner believes the choice to be made is sometimes secondary to the escape from indecision. Hence Skinner says "a problem to which a good deal of attention has been given arises when two or more responses appear to be possible and a person chooses or decides among them. The problem is to escape from indecision rather than to discover an effective response."[132] This process takes the following form according to Skinner:

> The individual manipulates relevant variables in mak-
> ing a decision because the behavior of doing so has
> certain reinforcing consequences. One of these is sim-
> ply escape from indecision. Conflicting alternatives
> lead to an oscillation between incomplete forms of
> response which, by occupying a good deal of the
> individual's time, may be strongly aversive. Any be-
> havior which brings this conflict to an end will be
> positively reinforced.[133]

From these remarks it can be seen that coming to a decision or solving a problem is not merely a matter of mentally discussing something with one's self. It is much more akin to dealing with one's self as one might deal with another. The solution desired is one which can lead to action. To achieve this is a matter of making one of the possible decisions more probable. This will be done by altering factors in the environment—since it is ultimately conditions outside the self which determine the probability of a given response. In discussing this point, Skinner says:

> The result of solving a problem is the appearance of a
> solution in the form of a response. The response alters
> the situation so that the problem disappears. The rela-
> tion between the preliminary behavior and the appear-
> ance of the solution is simply the relation between the
> manipulation of variables and the emission of a re-
> sponse.[134]

Skinner also agrees with Dewey that problem solving activity is so central to understanding human behavior that "since there is probably no behavioral process which is not relevant to the solving of some problem, an exhaustive analysis of techniques would coincide with an analysis of behavior as a whole."[135]

In dealing with moral problem solving in particular, Skinner points out that all of the problems which can be classified as conflicts between selves (and which were discussed above) can also be referred to as moral problems.[136] In these problems, it will be recalled, a self is thought of as a system of responses. Since a given individual may have more than one system of responses, it is always possible for these selves to come into conflict. The method of dealing with such moral problems would presumably be the same used in dealing with other types of problems. This process involves the manipulating of variables in the environment which will make a certain response more probable. Unlike Dewey, however, Skinner gives no indication of how this can best be done.

9. *Dewey and Skinner on Watson's Behaviorism*

The discussion of Skinner's behaviorism in this chapter has involved several comparisons of Skinner's views with those of Dewey. In this section, the behaviorism of both Skinner and Dewey will be contrasted with that of the founder of behaviorism, John B. Watson.[137]

Watson saw himself as originating psychology as a scientific discipline. All psychology which preceded his own he dismissed as being tainted with medieval conceptions of consciousness or the soul, and thus being unscientific. For example, Watson reports that "it was the boast of Wundt's students in 1879, when the first psychological laboratory was established, that psychology had at last become a science without a soul. For fifty years," he continues, "we have kept this pseudo-science, exactly as Wundt laid it down. All that Wundt and his students really accomplished was to substitute for the word 'soul' the word 'consciousness.'"[138]

In order to make psychology scientific, Watson effected a revision of its scope, purpose, methods, and vocabulary. Concerning these revisions, Watson says:

> In his efforts to get uniformity in subject matter and in methods the behaviorist began his own formulation of the problem of psychology by sweeping aside all medieval conceptions. He dropped from his scientific vocabulary all subjective terms such as sensation, perception, image, desire, purpose, and even thinking and emotion as they were subjectively defined.[139]

Further, he points out that:

> Psychology as the behaviorist views it is a purely objective experimental branch of natural science. Its theoretical goal is the prediction and control of behavior. Introspection forms no essential part of its methods, nor is the scientific value of its data dependent upon the readiness with which they lend themselves to interpretation in terms of consciousness. The behaviorist, in his efforts to get a unitary scheme of animal response, recognizes no dividing line between man and brute. The

behavior of man, with all its refinement and complexity, forms only a part of the behaviorist's total scheme of investigation.[140]

In his zeal to reform psychology, Watson was given to strong statements of his position and subsequently was often misunderstood.[141] His view of "consciousness," for example, was sometimes taken to be a denial that we possess anything answering to that name. Skinner, for example, states that "methodological behaviorism [Watson] could be said to ignore consciousness, feelings, and states of mind, but radical behaviorism [Skinner] does not...."[142] In a similar manner, Dewey claimed that "the chief objection to the narrower forms of behaviorism is that their obsession against the mental, because of previous false theories about it, shuts the door to ever entering upon inquiry."[143] Watson, however, did not deny that we possess consciousness. Rather, he merely denied that psychology could benefit from the introspective descriptions of consciousness which its long history had produced. As Watson states the point:

> The separate observation of 'states of consciousness' is... not more a part of the task of the psychologist than of the physicist. We might call this the return to a nonreflective and naive use of consciousness. In this sense consciousness may be said to be the instrument or tool with which all scientists work.... If you will grant the behaviorist the right to use consciousness in the same way that other natural scientists employ it—that is, without making consciousness a special object of observation—you have granted all that my thesis requires.[144]

Watson's primary complaint against the belief that consciousness is the subject matter of psychology, and introspection its method, is that the results of this approach in the past have been unreliable and unscientific.[145] Hence he notes:

> As a result of this major assumption that there is such a thing as consciousness and that we can analyze it by introspection, we find as many analyses as there are individual psychologists. There is no way of experimentally attacking and solving psychological problems and standardizing methods.[146]

On this score both Skinner and Dewey are in close agreement with Watson, as their positions, discussed previously, have made clear.

The two most significant points at which both Dewey and Skinner part with Watson concern the importance of physiology for psychology and the significance of classical (or what Skinner calls respondent) conditioning. Watson believed that all behavior could be reduced to instances of classical conditioning or stimulus-response reactions. Thus he says "behavioristic psychology has as its goal *to be able, given the stimulus, to predict the response—or, seeing the reaction take place to state what the stimulus is that has called out the reaction.*"[147] Dewey's criticism of this position has already been presented within the discussion of his article "The Reflex Arc Concept in Psychology," in Chapter Two. Skinner criticizes this notion on three counts.

The first, already noted above, involves Skinner's assertion that only a small percentage of our total activity can truly be placed under the heading of classical stimulus-response behavior. On this point Skinner says:

> We cannot, with Watson, define a response as 'anything the animal does, such as turning toward or away from a light, jumping at a sound, and more highly organized activities such as building a skyscraper, drawing plans, having babies, writing books and the like.' There is no reason to expect that responses of the latter sort will obey simple dynamic laws.[148]

The second point concerns Skinner's concept of operant conditioning and his analysis of behavior in terms of a three term contingency. Watson has no counterpart for these concepts in his analysis of behavior. Accordingly, Skinner states: "Every stimulus-response or input-output formulation of behavior suffers from a serious omission. No account of the interchange between organism and environment is complete until it includes the action of the environment upon the organism *after* a response has been made."[149]

The third objection points to the impracticality, from a scientific point of view, of trying to analyze all behavior in terms of mere stimulus-response reactions. Thus Skinner says

> Watson... defined the goal of psychological study as 'the ascertaining of such data and laws that, given the stimulus, psychology can predict what the response will

be; or, given the response, it can specify the nature of the
effective stimulus.' But a little reflection will show that
this is an impractical program. In the field of behavior
a science must contend with an extraordinary richness
of experimental material. The number of stimuli to
which a typical organism may respond originally is very
great.... 'It follows that the number of possible reflexes
is for all practical purposes infinite and that what one
might call the botanizing of reflexes will be a thankless
task.[150]

Concerning the importance of physiology in psychology, it was part
of Watson's contention that all of one's behaviors, including thinking,
have a physiological, and theoretically observable, base. Accordingly,
Watson claimed that

wherever there are thought processes...[there] are faint
contractions of the systems of musculature involved in
the overt exercise of the customary act, and especially
in the still finer systems of musculature involved in
speech.... Practically all natural thought goes on in
terms of sensorimotor processes in the larynx (but not in
terms of 'imageless thought') which rarely comes to
consciousness in any person....[151]

In commenting on this form of behaviorism, Dewey, after referring to
himself as a behaviorist, makes the following assertion:

In the first place, behavior is not viewed as something
taking place in the nervous system or under the skin of
an organism but always, directly or indirectly, in obvious overtness or at a distance through a number of
intervening links, an interaction with environing conditions. In the second place, other human beings who are
also acculturated are involved in the interaction, including even persons at a great distance in space and time,
because of what they have done in making the direct
environment what it is.[152]

Skinner's claim on this score is that eventually physiology may be
able to give explanations of behavior which significantly improve our

overall understanding of human psychology. At present, however, physiology is still in the early stages of this investigation. In the meantime, he claims, we can make significant progress in coming to understand behavior by focusing on its outward dimensions. Skinner points out that "the organism is, of course, not empty, and it cannot be adequately treated simply as a black box, but we must carefully distinguish between what is known about what is inside and what is merely inferred."[153] Further, he says:

> Physiology and, particularly with respect to behavior, neurology, have of course made great progress.... The nervous system is, however, much less accessible than behavior and environment, and the difference takes its toll. We know some of the processes which affect large blocks of behavior — sensory, motor, motivational, and emotional — but we are still far short of knowing precisely what is happening when, say, a child learns to drink from a cup, to call an object by its name, or to find the right piece of a jigsaw puzzle, as we are still far short of making changes in the nervous system as a result of which a child will do these things.[154]

Like Dewey and Skinner, Watson also was aware of the potential impact of a behavioristic psychology on ethical theory. He recognized, for example, that a more scientific account of human behavior was bound to lead to differences in the ways people behave. Accordingly, he says:

> I have attempted to show that while there is a science of psychology independent, interesting, worth while in itself, nevertheless to have a right to existence it must serve in some measure as a foundation for reaching out into human life. I think behaviorism does lay a foundation for saner living. It ought to be a science that prepares men and women for understanding the first principles of their own behavior.[155]

Watson recognized, however, that the role behaviorism may play in the organization and control of a culture may someday be much greater than it is today. At present, behaviorism may merely have the function of an instrument, used to carry out the appointed goals and tasks of others. However, the future may see behaviorism take a more active role in leadership. On this Watson states:

I would like to point out here that some time we will have a behavioristic ethics, experimental in type, which will tell us whether it is advisable from the standpoint of present and future adjustments of the individual to have one wife or many wives; to have capital punishment or punishment of any kind; whether prohibition or no prohibition; easy divorces or no divorces; whether many of our other prescribed courses of conduct make for adjustment of the individual or the contrary, such for example as having a family life or even knowing our own fathers and mothers.[156]

This chapter has presented an overview of Skinner's psychology and some of its implications. A number of similarities between the views of Dewey and Skinner have been brought out. For example, it was argued that in the case of such concepts as impulse and habit, the primary difference between the two men is verbal, not substantive. Further, it was noted that both Dewey and Skinner begin their examination of human psychology with an analysis of the organism and its interactions with its environment. Both men conclude their analyses, as will be developed more fully in the next chapter, with the general assertion that our moral or ethical behavior is not so much an individual accomplishment as an effect of the social environment to which we are and have been exposed.

In addition, it was shown in this chapter that both Dewey and Skinner understand the concept of a moral problem in the same way. Both men see such a problem as one arising from conflicting goals or ideals. While Dewey is concerned with the possibilities for the resolution of such problems, however, Skinner is primarily interested in accounting for their causes. Dewey sees their resolution in the choice of a self which is compatible with one alternative but not the other; Skinner sees their cause as the learning of incompatible repertoires of behavior. The context of moral problems is the general area of problem solving. Both Dewey and Skinner hold that an understanding of problem solving is central to the understanding of thought itself, moral or otherwise.

The chapter concluded with a discussion of the early behaviorism of Watson and the reactions of Dewey and Skinner to this form of behaviorism. It was shown that for Skinner, as well as Dewey, Watson's version of behaviorism is an oversimplification of the complex organism-environment interaction.

The next chapter will trace out some of the ethical implications of the psychological doctrines of Dewey and Skinner. In particular, the issue of social reform or behavioral technology will be discussed, as well as relevant aspects of the is-ought question. It will be argued that with respect to the latter issue, both Dewey and Skinner take dramatically nontraditional points of view, while, with respect to the former issue both men are in close accord, and hold that any scheme of social reform must begin with a restructuring of the environment, rather than with the moral individual as an isolated phenomenon.

Endnotes

[1] B. F. Skinner, "The Problem of Consciousness—A Debate," *Philosophy and Phenomenological Research* 27 (March 1967): 332.

[2] B. F. Skinner, *The Behavior of Organisms* (New York: Appleton-Century-Crofts, 1938), p. 3.

[3] B. F. Skinner, *About Behaviorism* (New York: Alfred A. Knopf, Inc., 1974), pp. 31-32.

[4] Ibid., p. 32.

[5] B. F. Skinner, *Science and Human Behavior* (New York: Macmillan Company, 1953), p. 31. Cf. B. F. Skinner, *Contingencies of Reinforcement: A Theoretical Analysis* (New York: Appleton-Century-Crofts, 1969), p. 83.

[6] Skinner does not consider himself a dualist, though he does not deny some status to mental events.

[7] Skinner, *Science and Human Behavior*, p. 35.

[8] Ibid., p. 33.

[9] Skinner, *The Behavior of Organisms*, p. 8.

[10] Skinner, *Science and Human Behavior*, pp. 41-42.

[11] Ibid., p. 17.

[12] B. F. Skinner, *Beyond Freedom and Dignity* (New York: Alfred A. Knopf, Inc., 1974), p. 184.

[13] Skinner, *Science and Human Behavior*, p. 6.

[14] Ibid., p 23.

[15] John Dewey, *A Common Faith* (New Haven: Yale University Press, 1934), p. 15.

[16] Ibid., p. 16.

[17] Skinner, *Science and Human Behavior*, p. 49.

[18] Ibid., p. 90.

[19] Ibid., p. 56.

[20] Skinner, *The Behavior of Organisms*, p. 19.

[21] Richard I. Evans, *B. F. Skinner: The Man and His Ideas* (New York: E. F. Dutton and Company, Inc., 1968), p. 19.

[22] Concerning the nature of operants Skinner further says: "We have seen that any unit of operant behavior is to a certain extent artificial. Behavior is the coherent, continuous activity of an integral organism" (Skinner, *Science and Human Behavior*, p. 119).

[23] Ibid., p. 107. See also, Skinner, *About Behaviorism*, p. 74.

[24] Skinner, *Science and Human Behavior*, p. 87.

[25] Ibid., p. 73.

[26] Ibid.

[27] Ibid., p. 87.

[28] Ibid., p. 173.

[29] Ibid., p. 175.

[30] Ibid., p. 108. See also, Skinner, *Contingencies of Reinforcement*, p. 7.

[31] Skinner, *Science and Human Behavior*, p. 125.

[32] Ibid., p. 224.

[33] Ibid., p. 71. See also, p. 69.

[34] B. F. Skinner and Charles B. Ferster, *Schedules* of *Reinforcement* (New York: Appleton-Century-Crofts, 1968).

[35] Skinner, *Science and Human Behavior*, pp. 111-112.

[36] Ibid., p. 112.

[37] Ibid., p. 26. Skinner points out that "the evolution of inherited forms of behavior is as plausible as the evolution of any function of the organism when reasonably stable" (B. F. Skinner, *Cumulative Record: A Selection of Papers*, 3rd edition *[New York: Appleton-Century-Crofts,* 1972; first published, 1959], p. 36.04).

[38] Skinner, *Science and Human Behavior*, p. 55

[39] Skinner, *About Behaviorism*, p. 207.

[40] Skinner, *Science and Human Behavior*, p. 83.

[41] Skinner, *Beyond Freedom and Dignity*, p. 120.

[42] Ibid., p. 176. Skinner traces the origin of superstitious behavior to this phenomenon. See Skinner, *Science and Human Behavior*, p. 55.

[43] Skinner, *Contingencies of Reinforcement*, pp. 175-176.

[44] Ibid., p. 175.

[45] Skinner, *About Behaviorism*, p. 33.

[46] Skinner, Science *and Human Behavior*, p. 157.

[47] Ibid., pp. 49-50.

[48] Skinner, *The Behavior of Organisms*, p. 11.

[49] Skinner, *About Behaviorism*, p. 150.

[50] Skinner, *Contingencies of Reinforcement*, p. 131.

[51] Skinner, *About Behaviorism*, pp. 73-74.

[52] Skinner, *Contingencies of Reinforcement*, p. 175.

[53] Skinner, *About Behaviorism*, pp. 73-74.

[54] Skinner, *Science and Human Behavior*, p. 64.

[55] Skinner, *Beyond Freedom and Dignity*, p. 196.

[56] Skinner, *Contingencies of Reinforcement*, p. 131.

[57] Skinner, *Science and Human Behavior*, p. 209.

[58] Ibid., p. 160.

[59] Ibid., p. 167.

[60] Ibid., p. 160.

[61] Evans, *Skinner: The Man and His Ideas*, p. 11.

[62] Skinner, *Science and Human Behavior*, p. 146.

[63] Skinner, *About Behaviorism*, p. 55.

[64] Ibid.

[65] Skinner, *Science and Human Behavior*, p. 88.

[66] Skinner, *Beyond Freedom and Dignity*, p. 204.

67 Ibid., pp. 204-205.

68 Skinner, *About Behaviorism*, p. 57.

69 Ibid.

70 Ibid., p. 56.

71 Skinner, *Science and Human Behavior*, p. 283.

72 Ibid., p. 285.

73 Skinner, *Beyond Freedom and Dignity*, p. 199.

74 Ibid.

75 Skinner, *Science and Human Behavior*, p. 284.

76 Ibid., p. 286. See also, Skinner, *About Behaviorism*, p. 149.

77 Skinner, *About Behaviorism*, pp. 149-150; *Beyond Freedom and Dignity*, p. 199.

78 Skinner, *About Behaviorism*, p. 153.

79 Ibid., p. 31.

80 Skinner, *Beyond Freedom and Dignity*, p. 192.

81 Skinner, *About Behaviorism*, p. 17.

82 Skinner, *Beyond Freedom and Dignity*, pp. 190-191.

83 Skinner, *About Behaviorism*, p. 118.

84 Ibid., p. 165.

85 Ibid., p. 104.

86 Ibid.

87 Ibid., pp. 103-104. Cf. Dewey's discussion of "mental trials" in Chapter Three.

88 Ibid., p. 190.

89 Ibid., p. 189.

90 Ibid., p. 190.

91 Ibid., pp. 180-181

92 Skinner, *Science and Human Behavior*, pp. 228-229. Skinner points out that

self-management is often represented as a direct manipulation of feelings and states of mind. A person is to change his mind, use his will power, stop feeling anxious, and love his enemies. What he actually does is change the world in which he lives. In both intellectual and ethical self management he analyzes contingencies and may exact and apply rules. But very little self-management in this sense could be learned in one lifetime. Hence the value of folk wisdom, rules of thumb, proverbs, maxims, and other rules to be followed to adjust more expediently to the contingencies they describe (Skinner, *About Behaviorism*, p. 177).

93 Skinner, *Science and Human Behavior*, p. 229.

94 Skinner, *About Behaviorism*, pp. 176-177.

95 Ibid., pp. 195-196.

96 Ibid., p. 195.

97 Ibid., p. 194.

98 Skinner, *Science and Human Behavior*, p. 333.

[99] Ibid., p. 345.

[100] Skinner, *Beyond Freedom and Dignity*, p. 175.

[101] Skinner, *Science and Human Behavior*, p. 324. See also, Skinner, *Beyond Freedom and Dignity*, pp. 109, 113.

[102] Skinner, *Beyond Freedom and Dignity*, p. 174. Skinner says "any list of values is a list of reinforcers-conditioned or otherwise" (Skinner, *Cumulative Record*, p. 33).

[103] Skinner says "the sheer control of nature is itself reinforcing" (Skinner, *Cumulative Record*, p. 152).

[104] Skinner, *Science and Human Behavior*, p. 325.

[105] Ibid., p. 328.

[106] Ibid.

[107] Skinner to Morris, 13 Oct. 1977.

[108] B. F. Skinner, *Walden Two* (New York: Macmillan Publishing Company, Inc., 1948). Of this book Skinner says: "Several years ago I spent a pleasant summer writing a novel called *Walden Two*. One of the characters, Frazier, said many things which I was not yet ready to say myself" (Skinner, *Cumulative Record*, p. 99).

[109] Skinner to Morris, 13 Oct. 1977.

[110] Ibid.

[111] Skinner does say, however, that "whether we like it or not, survival is the ultimate criterion. This is where, it seems to me, science can help—not in choosing a goal, but in enabling us to predict the survival value of cultural practices." (Skinner, *Cumulative Record*, p. 34). Also, he states: "The values I have occasionally recommended are transitional. Other things being equal, I am betting on the group whose practices make for healthy, happy, secure, productive, and creative people" (Ibid.).

[112] Skinner, *Beyond Freedom and Dignity*, p. 22.

[113] Skinner to Morris, 13 Oct. 1977.

[114] Ibid.

[115] Skinner, *Beyond Freedom and Dignity*, p, 81.

[116] Skinner states: "Man himself may be controlled by his environment, but it is an environment which is almost wholly of his own making" (Ibid., pp. 205-206).

[117] Skinner points out:

> The concept of freedom which has emerged as part of the cultural practice of our group makes little or no provision for recognizing or dealing with these kinds of control [i.e., positive reinforcement]. Concepts like 'responsibility' and 'rights' are scarcely applicable. We are prepared to deal with coercive measures, but we have no traditional recourse with respect to other measures which in the long run (and especially with the help of science) may be much more powerful and dangerous (Skinner, *Cumulative Record*, pp. 27-28).

[118] Skinner, *Beyond Freedom and Dignity*, p. 99.

[119] Ibid., pp. 42-43.

[120] Ibid., p. 29.

[121] Ibid., p. 32.

122 Ibid., p.58.

123 Ibid., p.53.

124 Ibid., p.47.

125 Ibid., pp. 96-97.

126 Ibid., p. 19.

127 Ibid., p. 76.

128 Ibid., p. 19.

129 Skinner, *About Behaviorism*, pp. 53-54.

130 Ibid., p. 111.

131 Ibid., p. 112.

132 Ibid.

133 Skinner, *Science and Human Behavior*, p. 244.

134 Ibid., p. 252.

135 Skinner, *Contingencies of Reinforcement*, p. 133.

136 Skinner, *Science and Human Behavior*, p. 444.

137 Skinner says of Watson:

> It was John B. Watson who made the first clear, if rather noisy, proposal that psychology should be regarded simply as a science of behavior. He was not in a very good position to defend it. He had little scientific material to use in his reconstruction. He was forced to pad his textbook with discussions of the physiology of receptor systems and muscles and with physiological theories which were at the time no more susceptible to proof than the mentalistic theories they were intended to replace. (Skinner, *Contingencies of Reinforcement*, p. 224).

138 John B. Watson, *Behaviorism* (New York, The People's Institute Publishing Company, Inc., 1924), p. 5.

139 Ibid., p. 6.

140 John B. Watson, "Psychology as the Behaviorist Views It," *Psychological Review* 20 (1913): 158.

141 Perhaps the most famous of Watson claims was the following:

> I should like to go one step further now and say "Give me a dozen healthy infants, well-formed and my own specified world to bring them up in and I 'll guarantee to take any one at random and train him to become any type of specialist I might select-doctor, lawyer, artist, merchant-chief and, yes beggar-man and thief, regardless of his talents, penchants, tendencies, abilities, vocations, and race of his ancestors." (Watson, Behaviorism, p. 82.).

142 Skinner, *About Behaviorism*, p. 219.

143 Dewey, "Conduct and Experience," p. 416.

144 Watson, "Psychology as the Behaviorist Views It," pp. 175-176.

145 Watson says, for example,

> to show how unscientific is the concept [of consciousness] look for a moment at William James' definition of psychology. 'Psychology is the description and expla-

nation of states of consciousness as such.' Starting with a definition which *assumes* what he starts out to prove, he escapes his difficulty by an *argumentum ad hominem*. (Watson, Behaviorism, p. 5).

[146] Ibid., p. 6.

[147] Ibid., p. 16.

[148] Skinner, *The Behavior of Organisms*, p. 42.

[149] Skinner, *Contingencies of Reinforcement*, p. 5.

[150] Skinner, *The Behavior of Organisms*, p. 10. Cf. Skinner, *Contingencies of Reinforcement*, p. 78.

[151] Watson, "Psychology as the Behaviorist Views It," p. 174.

[152] Dewey, "Experience, Knowledge and Value," p. 555.

[153] Skinner, *About Behaviorism*, p. 212.

[154] Ibid., p. 213.

[155] Watson, *Behaviorism*, pp. 247-248.

[156] Ibid., p. 7.

APPLICATIONS AND CONCLUSIONS

The discussion through the first four chapters of this study has led from Dewey's view of psychology to his ethics, and from Skinner's psychology to some of its ethical implications. In this concluding chapter, the foregoing discussion will form the basis for a consideration of two important problems relating to ethical theory. The first problem concerns the relation of so-called descriptive or nonevaluative statements to evaluative or normative statements. This problem is popularly termed, in philosophical literature, the "is-ought" question. The second problem concerns the implications of the positions taken by Dewey and Skinner on psychology and ethics when applied to the problem of social reform, or in contemporary terminology, behavioral technology.

1. Dewey and the Is-Ought Question

An ongoing issue among professional philosophers is whether and to what extent descriptive statements can be used to support evaluative statements in some logical sense of 'support.' This question has been characterized as "the central problem in moral philosophy."[1] On one side of the question are philosophers who believe that no set of descriptive statements alone can logically entail a conclusion which is evaluative. They sometimes term attempts to bridge the gap between descriptive and evaluative statements a commission of the "naturalistic fallacy," so-called by G. E. Moore. The proponents of this side of the question often trace their intellectual heritage to David Hume, who they claim was the originator of their point of view. This claim itself, however, has not stood without controversy.

On the other side of the controversy are a variety of philosophers who have attempted to work within the descriptive-evaluative dichotomy and bridge the gap between these two forms of statements. Although, as ordinarily formulated, the problem begins with the assumption that there are two distinct types of statements, descriptive and evaluative, at least two alternative positions are logically possible. First, all statements, including what are usually called descriptive statements, could contain evaluative elements. On this view, to call a statement descriptive or evaluative is to acknowledge a matter of degree, not kind. Taking evaluation in its broadest sense, to include all operations of selection and rejection for a purpose, this view holds that what seem to be the baldest statements of fact are themselves the results of some evaluation. This is the basis of Dewey's position. Second, all statements may be seen as either purely descriptive or translatable into descriptive statements. On this view, what are called value statements are actually confused or concealed formulations of descriptive statements. The latter view, as will be shown below, is Skinner's position.

In line with Dewey's general rejection of rigid dichotomies, he rejects the basic premise which generates the is-ought question. This premise states that the world is divided into facts and values and that these two categories are mutually exclusive. As a result of his unwillingness to accept this basic premise, the is-ought problem, as it is commonly understood, does not even arise for Dewey. That this is the case, however, may not at first be obvious. In Chapter Three, for example, it was noted that according to Dewey it is not legitimate to infer from a statement that something is or has been desired or valued to the conclusion that it is desirable or valuable. The inference, as Dewey points out, is no more legitimate than inferring from the fact that something was eaten to the conclusion that it is edible. The reasons are the same in both cases. To say that something is edible is to say that "we have a knowledge of its interactions with other things sufficient to enable us to foresee its probable effects when it is taken into the organism and produces effects there."[2] Similarly, when it is said that something is valuable, an hypothesis is put forth from which predictions may be inferred. The reason for claiming that something is valuable is related to the fact that it has been valued in the past; but, in addition, the conditions of the production of what has been valued and its consequences are also taken into account. Thus, not everything which has been valued will be valuable because of the specific contingencies involved in its production and its consequences. On this, Dewey points out that "the distinction between the 'is' in the sense of the object of casually emerging desire and the 'should be' of a desire framed in relation to actual conditions is a distinction which in any case is bound to offer itself as human beings grow in maturity and part with the childish disposition to 'indulge' every impulse as it arises."[3]

Given this account, Dewey seems to be saying that we cannot derive a value statement from a statement of fact. However, Dewey's point is not a logical one but an empirical one. The point of controversy in the is-ought question (in its usual interpretation) is, however, a logical rather than an empirical one. Hence, while on first consideration it sounds as if Dewey were siding with those who believe "ought" cannot logically be derived from "is," in actuality, Dewey has not accepted the basic supposition of fact-value separation which leads to the is-ought dispute and is thus discussing a separate and more fundamental issue.

To discover the reason for this it is necessary to understand Dewey's view of facts and values. It is a mistake, according to Dewey, to separate facts and values as though they were two distinct types of entities. On this Dewey says:

> Why has modern philosophy contributed so little to bring about an integration between what we know about the world and the intelligent direction of what we do? ...The cause resides in unwillingness to surrender two ideas formulated in conditions which both intellectually and practically were very different from those in which we now live. These two ideas... are that knowledge is concerned with disclosure of the characteristics of ante-cedent existences and essences, and that the properties of value found therein provide the authoritative standards for the conduct of life.[4]

The temptation to think of facts as antecedent realities leads to what Dewey calls the "spectator theory of knowledge." As noted in Chapter Two, the spectator theory of knowledge envisions the process of knowing as a passive reception by the mind of ready-made facts. Against this theory, Dewey claims that the process of knowing is itself an important compo-nent in determining what is finally known. It is for this reason that Dewey denies the possibility of raw or uninterpreted facts as forming the basis of knowledge. As Dewey points out, "things in their immediacy are unknown and unknowable, not because they are remote or behind some impen-etrable veil of sensation of ideas, but because knowledge has no concern with them."[5] It will be recalled from Chapter Two, that gaining knowledge of something, for Dewey, consists in attaching meanings to it. Hence, since the meanings are attached, and do not come ready-made with the thing in question, the prospect of gaining immediate knowledge of something is seen to be frustrated. As Dewey states the point, "qualities which we attribute to objects ought to be imputed to our own ways of experiencing them, and these in turn are due to the force of intercourse and custom."[6]

Further, when we do take note of something and begin the process of coming to know it by learning its connections with other things, we do so for a purpose. That purpose is involved in knowing is enough by itself, for Dewey, to rule out the prospect of immediate knowledge or bare facts. Hence, he says, "under all the captions that are called immediate knowledge, or self-sufficient certitude or belief, whether logical, esthetic or epistemological, there is something selected for a purpose, and hence not simple, not self-evident and not intrinsically eulogizable."[7] To refer to something as a fact is, for Dewey, to call out its meanings, and these in turn are the projected consequences of the thing in question when seen or used in interaction with other aspects of experience. Accordingly, Dewey points out that, "when we name an event, calling it fire [for example], we speak proleptically; we do not name an immediate event; we invoke a meaning, namely, the potential consequences of the existence."[8]

Once the purposive process of selection and rejection has begun (that is, the process of knowing) and we have attached meanings to objects, we can then speak of the qualities of objects as being immediately given. The mistake which other philosophers have made, according to Dewey, is to forget that what they refer to as immediate qualities are already the products of the knowing process and are not antecedent realities or bare facts. That is, facts are immediate only in the sense that we are not now conscious of the mediating factors, since they have become a part of our way of perceiving things.

When understood in Dewey's sense, the phenomenon of immediate qualities reveals an important insight. The long-standing philosophical tradition against which Dewey reacts has held that the sense qualities, color, taste, sound, smell, and touch are more fundamental or immediate than the affective qualities, fearful, ugly, beautiful. However, Dewey warns against the prejudice of assuming that some qualities as perceived are more immediate or fundamental than others. Colors, for example, are not more or less immediate than other features of objects such as their beauty or ugliness. This is a point of critical importance for Dewey, for it is the point which allows him to reject the fact-value dichotomy as it is usually understood. Accordingly, Dewey states:

> Interactions of things with the organism eventuate in
> objects perceived to be colored and sonorous. They also

result in qualities that make the object hateful or delightful. All these qualities, taken as directly perceived or enjoyed, are terminal effects of natural interactions. They are individualized culminations that give static quality to a network of changes. Thus "tertiary" qualities... those which, in psychological analysis, we call affectional and emotional, are as much products of the doings of nature as are color, sound, pressure, perceived size and distance. But their very consummatory quality stands in the way of using the things they qualify as signs of other things.[9]

And further:

Empirically, things are poignant, tragic, beautiful, humorous, settled, disturbed, comfortable, annoying, barren, harsh, consoling, splendid, fearful; and are such immediately and in their own right and behalf.... These traits stand in themselves on precisely the same level as colors, sounds, qualities of contact, taste and smell. Any criterion that finds the latter to be ultimate and "hard" data will, impartially applied, come to the same conclusion about the former.[10]

Given the above assessment of immediate knowledge, it can be seen why Dewey was not convinced by the proponents of the fact-value dichotomy. Both what are called facts and values arise in our experience out of the same ground and in the same fashion. Accordingly, Dewey says "the favoring of cognitive objects and their characteristics at the expense of traits that excite desire, command action and produce passion, is a special instance of a principle of selective emphasis which introduces partiality and partisanship into philosophy."[11] Values are not part of a separate realm from facts but are "naturalistically interpreted as intrinsic qualities of events in their consummatory reference."[12] Further, Dewey states that "moral experience reveal[s] traits of real things as truly as does intellectual experience...."[13] In general terms, Dewey points out that "'valuing' is *not* a special isolated type of act performed by a peculiar or unique agent, under conditions so unique that valuings and values can be understood in isolation from orders of fact not themselves of the 'value' kind."[14] In overview, it can be seen that it is Dewey's behavioristic interpretation of values, as discussed in Chapter Three, that allows him to dispose of the fact-value dichotomy. On this point, Dewey states:

> The separation alleged to exist between the "world of facts" and the "realm of values" will disappear from human beliefs only as valuation-phenomena are seen to have their immediate source in biological modes of behavior and to owe their concrete content to the influence of cultural conditions.[15]

Relating the above discussion specifically to the is-ought question, Dewey's position is this: Taken in immediacy, an object may be seen, for example, as both red and enjoyed. *To say it is red is not more factual than to say it is enjoyed.* Nor is a thing's being enjoyed a matter of inference while its being red is an item of direct cognition. However, valuing something goes beyond mere enjoyment of it. Valuing something involves taking steps necessary to procure or maintain the thing valued. Thus, Dewey points out: "In empirical fact, the measure of the value a person attaches to a given end is not what he *says* about its preciousness but the care he devotes to obtaining and using the *means* without which it cannot be obtained."[16] Expressed another way, to value the end without at the same time valuing the means necessary to the end is mere deception. To effectively value something, then, involves the relating, in a practical way, of facts and values. Thus, the question for Dewey becomes not how one can logically derive value or "ought" statements from fact or "is" statements, but rather how one can possibly hold any value or "ought" statement without at the same time accepting the fact or "is" statements which support it. On this point Dewey says

> evaluative judgments cannot be arrived at so as to be warranted without going outside the 'value field' into matters physical, physiological, anthropological, historical, socio-psychological, and so on. Only by taking facts ascertained in these subjects into account can we determine the conditions and consequences of given valuings."[17]

Further, Dewey notes that

> *evaluative* statements concern or have reference to what ends are to-be-chosen, what lines of conduct are to-be-followed, what policies are to-be-adopted. But is it

> morally necessary to state grounds or reasons for the
> course advised and recommended. These consist of
> matter-of-fact sentences reporting what has been and
> now is, as conditions, and of estimates of consequences
> that will ensue if certain of them are used as means. For
> in my opinion sentences about what *should* be done,
> chosen, etc., are sentences, propositions, judgments, *in
> the logical sense* of those words only as matter-of-fact
> grounds are presented in *support* of what is advised,
> urged, recommended to be done—that is, worthy of
> being done on the basis of the factual evidence avail-
> able.[18]

Summarized, Dewey's point is this: "The test of the validity of any
particular intellectual conception, measurement or enumeration is functional, its use in making possible the institution of interactions which yield
results in control of actual experiences of observed objects."[19]

In reference to "ought" and "is," then, Dewey's point is that "ought"
must be grounded within "is" to be truly "ought." Free floating values
without factually determined means to their accomplishment are not truly
values. In Dewey's words, "the 'ought' always rises from and falls back
into the 'is,' and... the 'ought' is itself an 'is,'—the 'is' of action."[20] And
again: "It is only because the 'ought' rests upon and expressed the 'is' that
it is something more than vague, ill-directed sentiment or rigid external
command."[21]

2. Skinner and the Is-Ought Question

Like Dewey, Skinner views the is-ought question as one arising
because of a misinterpretation of the nature of values. For Skinner, the
belief that values cannot be derived from facts rests on the assumption that
values are somehow the possessions of what he calls "autonomous man,"
the free self-causing self. According to the latter view, values are something we can choose independent of all factual considerations. In opposition to this view, Skinner proposes that what we call value statements are
actually convenient or shorthand ways of stating factual or empirically
measurable phenomena. Specifically, what are called value statements,
such as "You ought to tell the truth," are disguised references to contingencies which control behavior. Skinner analyzes "You ought to tell the truth"
as: "If you are reinforced by the approval of your fellow men, you will be
reinforced when you tell the truth."[22] As Skinner points out, "value is to

be found in the social contingencies maintained for purposes of control."[23] Thus there is, for Skinner, a direct connection between value statements and factual statements. Value statements, to be properly understood, must be translated into the factual statements of which they are the shorthand formulations. Thus for Skinner:

> "You ought to love your neighbor" may be converted into the two statements: (1) "The approval of your fellow men is positively reinforcing to you" and (2) "loving your fellow men is approved by the group of which you are a member," both of which may be demonstrated scientifically. The statement may also be used, of course, to coerce an individual into behaving in a fashion which resembles loving his neighbor, and indeed is probably most often used for this reason, but... this is not what is meant by a value judgment.[24]

Or again:

> A sentence beginning "You ought" is often a prediction of reinforcing consequences. "You ought to take an umbrella" may be taken to mean, "You will be reinforced for taking an umbrella." A more explicit translation would contain at least three statements: (1) Keeping dry is reinforcing to you; (2) carrying an umbrella keeps you dry in the rain; and (3) it is going to rain. All these statements are properly within the realm of science.[25]

Thus the connection between value statements (when used as such and not as disguised commands) and factual statements, can be expressed in terms of a general formula. For Skinner, value statements are not a separate kind of statement from statements of fact. Value statements, rather, form the basis of testable hypotheses. From a value statement, understood as a hypothesis, may be derived certain predictions which themselves are empirically testable. From statements asserting "You ought to do x," can be inferred the prediction "You will be reinforced for doing x." If the prediction is accurate, the individual will be reinforced for doing x, and his doing x will become more probable in the future.

From these comments it can be seen that for Skinner, as for Dewey, the significant question is not whether "ought" statements can logically be derived from "is" statements, but whether we can truly be said to understand "ought" statements without understanding the "is" statements from which they arise. It is only because philosophers have taken "ought" statements out of context and dealt with values as possessions of free and autonomous minds, that the is-ought question arose and has proved such a mystery.

As noted in Chapter Four, Skinner's analysis of value statements is based on his belief that they are "statement[s] made because of reinforcing consequences which arise either from genetic endowment or cultural contingencies."[26] However, Skinner does not intend this analysis of value statements to reflect what people ordinarily believe they mean when they make statements of the form "You ought to do x." Rather, as a metaethical analyst, his point is that if we are to make consistent sense of value statements we need to take them as implying predictions about reinforcing contingencies. Thus, it would not be a serious criticism of Skinner to point out that people do not intend, when they say, "You ought to do x," merely that you will be reinforced by the consequences of doing x. Skinner's contention is that to understand what value statements involve one must return to their primitive inception or biological basis and give a naturalistic account of them. Accordingly, Skinner says:

> Long before anyone formulated the "norm," people attacked those who stole from them. At some point stealing came to be called wrong and as such was punished even by those who had not been robbed. Someone familiar with these contingencies, possibly from having been exposed to them, could then advise another person: "Don't steal." If he had sufficient prestige or authority, he would not need to describe the contingencies further. The stronger form, "Thou shalt not steal," as one of the Ten Commandments, suggests supernatural sanctions. Relevant social contingencies are implied by "You ought not to steal," which could be translated, "If you tend to avoid punishment, avoid stealing," or "Stealing is wrong, and wrong behavior is punished."[27]

Resistance to this kind of interpretation of value statements is traced by Skinner to the fact that when we are able to "see" the variables which are controlling a person's behavior, we tend to give the person less credit or responsibility for his/her actions than when we are unaware of these causes. A knowledge of the variables of which a person's behavior is a function tends to rob a person of his freedom and dignity. Conversely, if we believe that a person is directed in his choices purely by internal and (in principle) unobservable forces, such as a will or moral sense, then we restore freedom and dignity to the individual. For Skinner, this price for freedom and dignity is too high. According to Skinner, if it is demeaning to human nature to propose that people respond to statements of the form "You ought to do x" out of fear of punishment or desire for reinforcement, rather than for any purely "moral" reasons, his interpretation at least has the advantage of opening the question to scientific investigation. Thus, while it may never be possible to construct an experiment such as that proposed in Plato's *Republic* in the story of the ring of Gyges, it is at least possible in principle that some evidence may be adduced for Skinner's position by less direct means. On the contrary, viewing value statements as having nothing to do with contingencies of reinforcement precludes forever the possibility of exposing questions of value to empirical investigation.

3. Social Reform and Behavioral Technology

From the preceding discussion it is clear that both Dewey and Skinner conceive of values as natural phenomena arising out of, but not reducible to, organic activity. Further, both men recognize that values are not personal or individual phenomena, but rather that values have an inescapable social dimension. On the social nature of values, Dewey states:

> These two facts, that moral judgment and moral responsibility are the work wrought in us by the social environment, signify that all morality is social; not because we *ought* to take into account the effect of our acts upon the welfare of others, but because of facts. Others *do* take account of what we do, and they respond accordingly to our acts. Their responses actually *do* affect the meaning of what we do.[28]

In a similar vein, Skinner points out that:

> People living together in groups come to control one another with a technique which is not inappropriately called "ethical." When an individual behaves in a fashion acceptable to the group, he receives admiration, approval, affection, and many other reinforcements

which increase the likelihood that he will continue to behave in that fashion. When his behavior is not acceptable, he is criticized, censured, blamed, or otherwise punished. In the first case the group calls him "good"; in the second, "bad."[29]

As a result of the recognition by both Dewey and Skinner of the social nature of values, it follows that the values personally espoused by both thinkers must themselves have social consequences. In addition, it is apparent that to understand and promote values in a social context is to promote a transformation of the social environment in which values themselves arise and are fostered. Consequently, since to advance the transformation of the social environment is to engage in social reform, or, in its contemporary appellation, behavioral technology, both Dewey and Skinner must be seen (as an implication of their analyses of values) to be engaged in such reform or technology.

Furthermore, both Skinner and Dewey, through their recognition of the formidable significance of science in general and psychology in particular for dealing with questions of ethical control, are unavoidably led to the conclusion that promotion of the transformation of the social environment must begin with an adequate understanding of the nature of the organism whose behavior is the ultimate concern in any attempt at social reform. In stressing the significance of scientific understanding for social reform, Skinner says

> the methods of science have been enormously success-
> ful wherever they have been tried. Let us then apply
> them to human affairs.... If we can observe human
> behavior carefully from an objective point of view and
> come to understand it for what it is, we may then be able
> to adopt a more sensible course of action.[30]

In addition, Dewey notes that the natural outcome of a behavioristically oriented psychology is necessarily an interest in control and thus in behavioral technology. "The advent," according to Dewey, "of a type of psychology which builds frankly on the original activities of man and asks how these are altered, requalified and reorganized in consequence of their exercise in specifically different environments brings with itself the experimental attitude, and thereby substitutes the interest in control for the interest in merely recording and what is called 'explaining.'"[31] That this is the case is particularly important for Dewey because, as he points out:

"In a world like ours where people are associated together, and where what one person does has important consequences for other persons, attempt to influence the action of other persons so that they will do certain things and not do other things is a constant function of life."[32]

For Dewey, as well as Skinner, the goals of social reform are not abstract ideals which are to be forced on a reluctant social order. Both men understand social reform to be an amplification of individual values and the natural forces operating among individuals. In Dewey's words: "To form a mind out of certain native instincts by selecting an environment which evokes them and directs their course; to re-form social institutions by breaking up habits and giving peculiar intensity and scope to some impulse is the problem of social control in its two phases."[33] Skinner believes that the goal of social reform is to develop within a culture "a set of contingencies of reinforcement under which members behave in ways which maintain the culture, enable it to meet emergencies, and change it in such a way that it will do these things even more effectively in the future."[34]

Presently existing cultures are, for the most part, not the results of specific plans of behavioral technology. As Skinner points out:

> So far, men have designed their cultures largely by guesswork, including some very lucky hits; but we are not far from a stage of knowledge in which this can be changed. The change does not require that we be able to describe some distant state of mankind toward which we are moving or "deciding" to move. Early physical technology could not have foreseen the modern world, though it led to it. Progress and improvement are local changes. We better ourselves and our world as we go.[35]

Skinner, then, does not accept the idea that social reform must be patterned after a finalized master plan. Similarly, Dewey, in speaking of social reform as it would manifest itself as an educative process, denies the necessity of a finalized goal toward which reform must proceed. According to Dewey,

> even when the processes of education do not aim at the unchanged perpetuation of existing institutions, it is assumed that there must be a mental picture of some desired end, personal and social, which is to be at-

tained, and that this conception of a fixed determinate end ought to control educative processes. Reformers share this conviction with conservatives....An experimental social method would probably manifest itself first of all in surrender of this notion. Every care would be taken to surround the young with the physical and social conditions which best conduce, as far as freed knowledge extends, to release of personal potentialities. The habits thus formed would have entrusted to them the meeting of future social requirements and the development of the future state of society.[36]

As Skinner is acutely aware, the very notion of a planned or designed culture arouses grave suspicions in many people.[37] To the popular mind, a designed culture is synonymous with a totalitarian society marked by oppression and lack of freedom. However, as Skinner states:

The danger of the misuse of power is possibly greater than ever. It is not allayed by disguising the facts. We cannot make wise decisions if we continue to pretend that human behavior is not controlled, or if we refuse to engage in control when valuable results might be forthcoming. Such measures weaken only ourselves leaving the strength of science to others. The first step in a defense against tyranny is the fullest possible exposure to controlling techniques.[38]

As pointed out in Chapter Four, there is no question for Skinner whether we shall live in a controlled or uncontrolled environment. "We are all controlled," Skinner points out, "by the world in which we live, and part of that world has been and will be constructed by men. The question is this: Are we to be controlled by accident, by tyrants, or, by ourselves in effective cultural designs."[39] With some irony, Skinner says, "many of the things we value have emerged from the clash of ignorant armies on darkling plains, but it is not therefore wise to encourage ignorance and darkness."[40]

As already noted, part of the difficulty which many people have with the concept of cultural design arises from the equating of a design with a prearranged and fixed plan. But as Skinner attests:

Designing a new culture is in many ways like designing an experiment.... We cannot be sure that the practices we specify will have the consequences we predict, or that the consequences will reward our efforts. This is in the nature of such proposals. They are not value judgments—they are guesses. To confuse and delay the improvement of cultural practices by quibbling about the word *improve* is itself not a useful practice. Let us agree, to start with, that health is better than illness, wisdom better than ignorance, love better than hate, and productive energy better than neurotic sloth.[41]

Dewey, also, was aware that effective social reform must take the form of experimentation. He notes that

policies and proposals for social action [should] be treated as working hypotheses, not as programs to be rigidly adhered to and executed. They will be experimental in the sense that they will be entertained subject to constant and well-equipped observation of the consequences they entail when acted upon, and subject to ready and flexible revision in the light of observed consequences.[42]

Like Skinner, however, Dewey was also aware that "men have got used to an experimental method in physical and technical matters... [but] are still afraid of it in human concerns."[43]

A central issue involved in social reform or behavioral technology is how best to influence or control the behavior of others, and thereby to implement the desired values. For both Dewey and Skinner the traditional methods for approaching this problem have been inadequate or inefficient. As noted in Chapter Four, Skinner is critical of the institution of punishment as a means of social control, primarily because of its undesirable side effects. Punishment leads to behavior involving escape and avoidance and to aggression toward the punishing agency. On this same topic Dewey states:

A threat may, for example, prevent a person from doing something to which he is naturally inclined by arousing fear of disagreeable consequences if he persists. But he may be left in the position which exposes him later on to influences which will lead him to do even worse things. His instincts of cunning and slyness may be aroused, so that things henceforth appeal to him on the side of evasion and trickery more than would otherwise have been the case.[44]

Aside from punishment and threats, other traditional methods of control involve trying to deal directly with the mind of an individual, as in a preacher's moral exhortation, which Dewey calls "that deadest of all dead things."[45] The difficulty with such direct methods as exhortation or moralizing is that they presuppose a false mentalistic psychology. According to the traditional mentalistic analysis, to change a person's behavior, one first deals directly with a person's mind or rational faculty. This rational faculty or mind (so it is assumed) causes or results in the desired outward behavior. Change a person's mind by reason or emotion and his behavior will follow suit. The belief in this psychology is, for Skinner, a belief in what he calls *autonomous man*. "Autonomous man," he says, "is a device used to explain what we cannot explain in any other way. He has been constructed from our ignorance, and as our understanding increases, the very stuff of which he is composed vanishes."[46] On this same issue, Dewey gives the following analysis:

> When the self is regarded as something complete within itself, then it is readily argued that only internal moralistic changes are of importance in general reform. Institutional changes are said to be merely external.... The result is to throw the burden for social improvement upon free-will in its most impossible form.... Individuals are led to concentrate in moral introspection upon their own vices and virtues, and to neglect the character of the environment.... Let us perfect ourselves within, and in due season changes in society will come of themselves is the teaching.... But when self-hood is perceived to be an active process it is also seen that social modifications are the only means of the creation of changed personalities. Institutions are viewed in their educative effect: — with reference to the types of individuals they foster. The interest in individual moral improvement and the social interest in objective reform of economic and political conditions are identified.... We are led to ask what the specific stimulating, fostering and nurturing power of each specific social arrangement may be.[47]

In addition, as Dewey points out:

> The ultimate refuge of the standpatter in every field, education, religion, politics, industrial and domestic life, has been the notion of an alleged fixed structure of mind. As long as mind is conceived as an antecedent and ready-made thing, institutions and customs may be regarded as its offspring. By its own nature the ready-made mind works to produce them as they have existed and now exist.[48]

The breakdown in this mentalistic model for psychology becomes apparent when one considers the naturalistic basis of moral development. As Dewey asserts, our moral values are learned not through instruction *per se*, but through the environmental contingencies in which the instruction takes place. Dewey says

> children are surrounded by adults who constantly pass judgments of value on conduct. And these comments are not coldly intellectual; they are made under conditions of strongly emotional nature.... The attitudes remain when the circumstances of their origin are forgotten; they are made so much a part of the self that they seem to be inevitable and innate.... The very fact of the early origin and now unconscious quality of the attendant [moral] intuitions is often distorting and limiting. It is almost impossible for later reflection to get at and correct that which has become unconsciously part of the self.[49]

For Dewey and Skinner the consequence of these criticisms of mentalistic psychology is clear. If people's behavior is to be altered, this will not effectively be accomplished through the direct attempt to change minds. Instead, the more indirect route of altering the environment in which people live must be prescribed. As Dewey explains,

> the effective control of their [people's] powers is not through precepts, but through the regulation of their conditions. If this regulation is to be not merely physical or coercive, but moral, it must consist of the intelligent selection and determination of the environments in

which we act; and in an intelligent exaction of responsibility for the use of men's powers.[50]

Further, he asserts that "there is not in fact, any such thing as the direct
influence of one human being on another apart from use of the physical
environment as an intermediary."[51] Or again he says, "we cannot change
habit directly: that notion is magic. But we can change it indirectly by
modifying conditions, by an intelligent selecting and weighing of the
objects which engage attention and which influence the fulfillment of
desires."[52]

Concurring with Dewey on the indirect nature of control, Skinner
points out that

> the organism becomes a person as it acquires a
> repertoire of behavior under the contingencies of
> reinforcement to which it is exposed during its life-
> time. The behavior it exhibits at any moment is under
> the control of a current setting. It is able to acquire
> such a repertoire under such control because of pro-
> cesses of conditioning which are also part of its
> genetic endowment.[53]

And again:

> It is no doubt valuable to create an environment in which
> a person acquires effective behavior rapidly and contin-
> ues to behave effectively. In constructing such an envi-
> ronment we may eliminate distractions and open
> opportunities, and these are key points in the metaphor
> of guidance or growth and development; but it is the
> contingencies we arrange, rather than the unfolding of
> some predetermined pattern, which are responsible for
> the changes observed.[54]

The practical manner of effecting social reform, then, for both Dewey
and Skinner, is through the medium of the contingencies in the environment. To change people one must first change the world in which they
grow and live, not the other way around. Proposing this insight into social
reform is not an original contribution to moral thought by either Dewey or
Skinner. Plato had the same basic insight in the *Republic*. However, with
the displacement of mentalistic psychology and the advent of a behavior-

istic view of psychology, the means for effectively carrying out this insight are now genuinely available, whereas for Plato they were not.

4. Summary and Conclusions

It has been the goal of this study to analyze the behavioristic context of Dewey's ethics. In carrying out this analysis it has been necessary to trace both the factors leading to Dewey's understanding of the behavioristic context of ethics and those factors consequent upon this understanding. Among the factors discussed which were instrumental in leading Dewey to his belief that ethics must be grounded within a behavioristic framework were: (1) his view of the nature of science, (2) his general rejection of dichotomies and dualisms, (3) his belief that human experience cannot adequately be understood as the product of independent human agencies carrying out independent individual lives, as well as (4) his recognition of the unproductiveness of mentalistic psychologies as foundations for ethical thought. In addition, it was shown that while Dewey had not always recognized the significance of behavioristic psychology for ethical theory, this recognition came early in his professional career. Dewey, it was shown, was influenced by and critical of both the reflex arc concept in psychology and the originator of behaviorism, John B. Watson. Further, the study has pointed to the fact that what Dewey saw fit to accept or reject in the teachings of Watson were closely paralleled by the reactions of the later behaviorist B. F. Skinner.

In preparation for the exposition of Dewey's views on ethics proper, the central lines of his psychology were developed. The main concepts in Dewey's psychology were discussed, including: the organism and its environment, impulse, habit, character, and intelligence. The specific discussion of Dewey's ethics included considerations of the moral situation, ends-in-view, the role of moral judgments as hypotheses, and the significance of sympathy in ethical thought.

In order that Dewey's views of the behavioristic context of ethics might be put in perspective, the study included a synoptic view of the writings of B. F. Skinner on psychology and its relations to ethics. The discussion presented some of the changes in behaviorism, as a philosophy of psychology, from its inception with Watson to its contemporary stature as a significant analysis of the role of psychological theory. In addition, where important parallels were drawn between the views of Skinner and those of Dewey on psychology and its importance for ethics. The study traced the fact that in many general respects, Dewey anticipated certain of

Skinner's insights, especially on questions relating to the ethical or moral implications of a behavioristic analysis of human behavior.

Finally, the study dealt briefly with two important ethical issues from the perspective of ethics in a behavioristic context: the is-ought question and the problem of social reform. It was suggested that in the case of both of these difficult and important ethical issues, the positions of both Dewey and Skinner lead them to an acceptance of many of the same conclusions.

At least five important general conclusions can be drawn from the information presented in this study and the significance of these conclusions at least partially justifies the study as a whole.

The first general conclusion is that many of the problems with which traditional ethical theorists struggle are problems only because of the acceptance of a false or misleading psychological premise, specifically the acceptance of mentalism or the belief in mind or self as a given antecedent reality rather than a biological-historical product in process.

The second general conclusion suggests that the intellectual or logical connection between behaviorism, on the one hand, and pragmatism, on the other, is neither incidental nor coincidental. Behaviorism can be seen as pragmatic analysis applied to matters psychological; whereas pragmatism, when confronted with questions of human behavior and its control, leads to a behavioristic philosophy psychology.

The third general conclusion results from a comparison of the views of Dewey and Skinner regarding psychology and ethics. This conclusion consists in the proposition that, given a behavioristic foundation or set of suppositions, certain ethical positions follow with some necessity. Among these are: (1) the rejection of the fact-value dichotomy as a rigid division, (2) the recognition that values can be traced to organic or biological sources, (3) the rejection of mental "intuitions" as warranted reasons in ethical reasoning, and (4) seeing the sources of ethical control to be within our environment rather than merely within ourselves.

The fourth general conclusion may be seen to overlap or encompass parts of the three conclusions already mentioned. This conclusion involves making explicit a central theme which can be found throughout Dewey's ethical writings. This theme can be expressed by saying that for Dewey ethical experience rests within and rises from a shared common base of values. In Dewey's earliest writings the common base of values was related to an idealistic conception of the Absolute. Throughout most of his writings, however, this common base of values grows out of the fact that, before anything else, people are organisms. As organisms individuals interact with their environment. However, as human organisms individuals influence one another and in turn are influenced by one another. This constant interchange creates a social environment not common to all organic life. Central to this social environment is the institution of language and in particular the use of language for control. Within the social environment, the values which originated from organic sources take on a *life of their own,* and are transmitted to new generations as they arise. It is because values are taken up and perpetuated by the social environment that the enterprise of ethics (or philosophy considered as criticism) becomes necessary. This is the case, for as each new generation arises the customs with which it is confronted represent the results of attempts by prior generations to resolve specific organic impulses within their own social and physical environments. However, as these environments change, customs or values to be effective must also change and be adapted.

Finally, the fifth general conclusion concerns the positive service rendered for ethical theory by both Dewey and Skinner. While, as noted in the first chapter, philosophers since Plato have been aware that their views of human nature were important to their views on ethics, both Dewey and Skinner attempted to make the elements of this relationship explicit. By so doing they promoted considerations of ethics from a scientific or empirical point of view and thereby gave new substance to the dictum "ought implies can." Both Dewey and Skinner have helped to show that the greater our knowledge of human psychology the better able we will be to deal with matters of ethical concern.

Endnotes

[1] W. D. Hudson, ed., *The Is-Ought Question* (New York: St. Martin's Press, 1969), p. 11.

[2] Dewey, *The Quest for Certainty*, p. 266.

[3] Dewey, *Theory of Valuation*, p. 32.

[4] Dewey, *The Quest for Certainty*, p. 71.

[5] Dewey, *Experience and Nature*, p. 86.

[6] Ibid., p. 14.

[7] Ibid., p. 30.

[8] Ibid., p. 191.

[9] Dewey, *The Quest for Certainty*, p. 239.

[10] Dewey, *Experience and Nature*, p. 96.

[11] Ibid., pp. 24-25.

[12] Ibid., p. xvi.

[13] Ibid., p. 19.

[14] Dewey, "The Field of 'Value,'" p. 68.

[15] Dewey, *Theory of Valuation*, p. 64.

[16] Ibid., p. 27; see also pp. 14-15. See also, Dewey, "The Field of 'Value,'" p. 67.

[17] Dewey, "The Field of 'Value,'" p. 77.

[18] John Dewey, "Ethical Subject Matter and Language," *Journal of Philosophy* 42 (Dec. 20, 1945): 711.

[19] Dewey, *The Quest for Certainty*, p. 129.

[20] John Dewey, "Moral Theory and Practice," p. 105.

[21] Ibid., p. 108.

[22] Skinner, *Beyond Freedom and Dignity*, p. 112.

[23] Ibid.

[24] Skinner, *Science and Human Behavior*, p. 429.

[25] Ibid.

[26] Skinner to Morris, 13 Oct. 1977.

[27] Skinner, *Beyond Freedom and Dignity*, p. 114.

[28] Dewey, *Human Nature and Conduct*, p. 316.

[29] Skinner, *Cumulative Record*, p. 25.

[30] Skinner, *Science and Human Behavior*, p. 5.

[31] Dewey, "The Need for Social Psychology," p. 274.

[32] Dewey and Tufts, *Ethics* (1932), p. 323.

[33] Dewey, "The Need for Social Psychology," p. 269.

[34] Skinner, *Contingencies of Reinforcement*, p. 41.

[35] Skinner, *Cumulative Record*, p. 36.11.

[36] Dewey, *The Public and Its Problems*, pp. 200-201.

[37] See, for example, Skinner, *About Behaviorism*, Chapter 1.

[38] Skinner, *Cumulative Record*, p. 11.

[39] Ibid., pp. 10-11.

[40] Ibid., p. 12.

[41] Ibid., p. 6.

[42] Dewey, *The Public and Its Problems*, pp. 202-203.

[43] Ibid., p. 169.

[44] Dewey, *Democracy and Education*, p. 31.

[45] Dewey, "Moral Theory and Practice," p. 102.

[46] Skinner, *Beyond Freedom and Dignity*, p. 200.

[47] Dewey, *Reconstruction in Philosophy*, pp. 196-197.

[48] Dewey, "The Need for Social Psychology," p. 273.

[49] Dewey and Tufts, *Ethics* (1932), pp. 293-294.

[50] Dewey, *The Influence of Darwin on Philosophy*, p. 74.

[51] Dewey, *Democracy and Education*, p. 33.

[52] Dewey, *Human Nature and Conduct*, p. 20.

[53] Skinner, *About Behaviorism*, p. 207.

[54] Skinner, *Beyond Freedom and Dignity*, p. 88.

APPENDIX

603 Glenview Drive
Carbondale, Ill. 62901

October 3, 1977

Professor B. F. Skinner
Department of Psychology
Harvard University
Cambridge, Massachusetts

Dear Professor Skinner:

I am writing to you regarding some research I am doing.
I am a Ph.D. candidate at Southern Illinois University,
Carbondale, Illinois and am engaged in writing a dissertation for the Philosophy Department. In the dissertation
certain aspects of your writings are being favorably compared to relevant aspects in the writings of John Dewey.
Specifically, I am interested in the relations or interrelations which exist between ethical and psychological
matters. My thesis deals with the way in which psychological assumptions (such as the many mentalistic assumptions
to which you refer in your writings) affect ethical beliefs
and ethical theory.

Like yourself, Dewey was explicitly aware of the
significance of psychological presuppositions for ethical
discussion. Though his primary interests were in questions
of ethics and social philosophy, rather than psychology, he
took pains to examine his own psychological assumptions and
make them, as far as possible, correspond to the best available information. In his later writings especially, his
psychological assumptions were anti-mentalistic, and in
fact he referred to himself as a behaviorist and shared
many of the general beliefs of the behavioristic philosophy
you espouse.

In your writings I have found a like concern to follow
out purely psychological considerations to their potential
ethical implications. In particular I have noticed that
you are able to account for the psychological sources of
many contemporary ethical difficulties, as well as the
psychological basis of many individual moral dilemmas.
For example, in your discussions of the self (or selves)
you point out the source of conflicts between selves--

such as the man (in Science and Human Behavior) with conflicting repertoires of behavior--one relating to a business environment, the other to a religious environment. You present similar examples in Beyond Freedom and Dignity, p. 199, and in About Behaviorism, pp. 149-50. In Science and Human Behavior, p. 444, you point out that conflicts such as these can also be seen as moral problems.

My first question is whether you see this form of personal difficulty as arising because of aversive controlling measures or could similar problems arise in a culture which relied exclusively on non-aversive measures of control? As a follow-up question, do you suspect that the elimination of such problems can be achieved only through wholesale changes in the social environment, a la Walden Two, or do you feel science or ethics can offer individuals in our present social environment formulae, tools, or wisdom to enable them to deal with such problems individually?

My third question is whether you believe that as behavioristic principles become more widely accepted in our society the need for ethical theory will become less important? That is, as people are less inclined to ask questions of moral responsibility, will the examination and clarification of ethical justifications for certain courses of action become less important?

Finally, when you say that we should make the world less punishing (Beyond Freedom and Dignity, p. 81), do you see this as a value judgment, or is such a statement, as far as you are concerned, an empirical or scientific matter?

I would greatly appreciate any assistance you might give me with these questions. Thank you.

Yours truly,

Donald Morris

172

HARVARD UNIVERSITY
DEPARTMENT OF PSYCHOLOGY AND SOCIAL RELATIONS

WILLIAM JAMES HALL
33 KIRKLAND STREET
CAMBRIDGE, MASSACHUSETTS 02138

October 13, 1977

Mr. Donald Morris
603 Glenview Drive
Carbondale, Ill 62901

Dear Mr. Morris:

I have time for only the briefest answers to your interesting questions.

1. I think there could be difficult problems concerning the control of behavior by potential despots even though positive techniques are used.

2. I think progress could be made both by the organization of small communities and by "nibbling" at cultural practices in general -- as in education, therapy and so on.

3. I do not think that a more effective technology will eliminate the need to ask questions concerning moral responsibility though the questions will be phrased differently.

4. I do not interpret a value judgement as anything more than a statement made because of reinforcing consequences which arise either from genetic endowment or cultural contingencies.

Yours sincerely,

B. F. Skinner

BFS/sh

BIBLIOGRAPHY

1. Books

Adams, George P. and Montague, William Pepperell, eds. *Contemporary American Philosophy*. Series 2. New York: New York University Press, 1930.

Coughlan, Neil. *Young John Dewey: An Essay in American Intellectual History*. Chicago: The University of Chicago Press, 1973.

Dewey, John. *A Common Faith*. New Haven: The Yale University Press, 1934.

_____. *Art as Experience*. New York: Minton, Balch and Company, 1934.

_____. *Democracy and Education*. New York: The Macmillan Company, 1916.

_____. *Experience and* Nature. Chicago: Open Court Publishing Company, 1925. Second edition, with a preface, London: G. Allen and Unwin, 1929; reprint of the second edition, New York: Dover Publications Inc., 1958.

_____. *Human Nature and Conduct*. New York: Henry Holt and Company, 1922.

_____. *Logic: The Theory of Inquiry*. New York: Henry Holt and Company, 1938.

_____. *Outlines of a Critical Theory of Ethics*. Ann Arbor, Mich.: Register Publishing Company, 1891.

_____. *Philosophy and Civilization*. New York: Minton, Balch and Company, 1931.

_____. *Psychology*. New York: Harper and Brothers, 1887. *[The Early Works of John Dewey, 1882-1898*, ed. George E. Axtelle, et al., vol. 2. Carbondale and Edwardsville: Southern Illinois University Press, 1967.]

_____. *Reconstruction in Philosophy*. New York: Henry Holt and Company, 1920; Boston: The Beacon Press, 1948, enlarged edition with new introduction.

_____. *Theory of Valuation. International Encyclopedia of Unified Science*, vol. 2, no. 4. Chicago: University of Chicago Press, 1939.

_____. *The Influence of Darwin Upon Philosophy and Other Essays in Contemporary Thought*. New York: Henry Holt and Company, 1910.

_____. *The Problems of Men*. New York: Philosophical Library, 1946.

_____. *The Public and Its Problems*. New York: Henry Holt and Company, 1927.

_____. *The Quest for Certainty*. New York: Minton, Balch and Company, 1929.

_____. *The Study of Ethics: A Syllabus*. Ann Arbor, Mich.: Register Publishing Company, 1891. [*The Early Works of John Dewey, 1882-1898*, ed. George E. Axtelle, et al., vol. 4. Carbondale and Edwardsville: Southern Illinois University Press, 1971.]

Dewey, John, and Tufts, James H. *Ethics*. New York: Henry Holt and Company, 1908.

_____. *Ethics*. Second edition, revised. New York: Henry Holt and Company, 1932.

Dykhuizen, George. *The Life and Mind of John Dewey*. Carbondale and Edwardsville: Southern Illinois University Press, 1973.

Evans, Richard I. *B. F. Skinner: The Man and His Ideas*. New York: E. P. Dutton and Company, Inc., 1968.

Hudson, W. D., ed. *The Is-Ought Question*. New York: St. Martin's Press, 1969.

Lepley, Ray, ed. *Value: A Cooperative Inquiry*. New York: Columbia University Press, 1949.

McDermott, John J., ed. *The Philosophy of John Dewey*. Vols. 1 and 2. New York: G. P. Putnam's Sons, 1973.

Murchison, Carl, ed. *Psychologies of 1930*. Worcester, Mass.: Clark University Press, 1930.

Schilpp, Paul Arthur, ed. *The Philosophy of John Dewey*. "The Library of Living Philosophers," vol. 1. Evanston and Chicago: Northwestern University, 1939; LaSalle, IL: The Open Court Publishing Company, second edition, 1951.

Skinner, B. F. *About Behaviorism*. New York: Alfred A. Knopf, Inc., 1974.

_____. *Beyond Freedom and Dignity*. New York: Alfred A. Knopf, Inc., 1971.

_____. *Contingencies of Reinforcement: A Theoretical Analysis*. New York: Appleton-Century-Crofts, 1969.

_____. *Cumulative Record*. New York: Appleton-Century-Crofts, 1959.

_____. *Particulars of My Life*. New York: McGraw-Hill Book Company, 1976.

_____. *Science and Human Behavior*. New York: Macmillan Company, 1953.

_____. *The Behavior of Organisms*. New York: Appleton-Century-Crofts, 1938.

_____. *Walden Two*. New York: Macmillan Company, 1948.

Watson, John B. *Behaviorism*. New York: The People's Institute Publishing Company, Inc., 1924.

2. Articles

Dewey, John. "Ethical Subject Matter and Language." *Journal of Philosophy* 42 (Dec. 20, 1945): 701-712.

_____. "Ethics and Physical Science," *Andover Review* 7 (June 1887): 573-91. [*The Early Works of John Dewey, 1882-1898*, ed. George E. Axtelle, et al., vol. 1. Carbondale and Edwardsville: Southern Illinois University Press, 1969.]

_____. "Moral Theory and Practice." *International Journal of Ethics* 2 (Jan. 1891): 186-203. *The Early Works of John Dewey. 1882-1898*, ed. George E. Axtelle, et al., vol. 3. Carbondale and Edwardsville: Southern Illinois University Press, 1969.]

_____. "Psychological Method in Ethics," *Psychological Review* 10 (Mar. 1903): 158-160.

_____. "Psychology as Philosophic Method." *Mind* 11 Apr.. 1886): 153-73. [*The Early-Works of John Dewey, 1882-1898*, ed. George E. Axtelle, et al., vol 1. Carbondale and Edwardsville: Southern Illinois University Press, 1969.]

_____. "The Need for Social Psychology." *Psychological Review* 24 (July 1917): 266-277.

_____. "The New Psychology." *Andover Review* 2 (Sept. 1884): 278-289. [*The Early Works of John* Dewey, *1882-1898,* ed. George E. Axtelle, et al., vol. 1. Carbondale and Edwardsville: Southern Illinois University Press, 1969.]

_____. "The Psychological Standpoint." *Mind* 11 (Jan. 1886): 1-19. [*The Early Works of John Dewey, 1882-1898*, ed. George E. Axtelle, et al., vol. 1. Carbondale and Edwardsville: Southern Illinois University Press, 1969.]

_____. "The Reflex Arc Concept in Psychology." *Psychological Review* 3 (July 1896): 357-70. [*The Early Works of John Dewey, 1882-1898*, ed. George E. Axtelle, et al., vol. 5. Carbondale and Edwardsville: Southern Illinois University Press, 1972.]

_____. "The Theory of Emotion." *Psychological Review* 1 (Nov. 1894): 553-69; 2 (Jan. 1895): 13-32. [*The Early Works of John Dewey, 1882-1898*, ed. George E.. Axtelle, et al., vol. 4. Carbondale and Edwardsville: Southern Illinois University Press, 1971.]

Skinner, B. F. "The Problem of Consciousness — A Debate." *Philosophy and Phenomenological Research* 27 (March 1967): 325-333.

Watson, John B. "Psychology as the Behaviorist Views It." *Psychological Review* 20 (1913): 158-177.

❦

INDEX